CUSTOMER SERVICE TRAINING

SECOND EDITION

Renée Evenson

AMACOM

AMERICAN MANAGEMENT ASSOCIATION

New York • Atlanta • Brussels • Chicago • Mexico City • San Francisco
Shanghai • Tokyo • Toronto • Washington, D. C.

Bulk discounts available. For details visit:
www.amacombooks.org/go/specialsales
Or contact special sales:
Phone: 800-250-5308
Email: specialsls@amanet.org
View all the AMACOM titles at: www.amacombooks.org

Library of Congress Cataloging-in-Publication Data
Evenson, Renee, 1951-
    Customer service training 101 : quick and easy techniques that get great results / Renee Evenson. —2nd ed.
        p. cm.
    Includes bibliographical references and index.
    ISBN-13: 978-0-8144-1641-9 (alk. paper)
    ISBN-10: 0-8144-1641-1 (alk. paper)
    1. Customer services. 2. Customer relations. 3. Employees--Training of. I. Title.
    HF5415.5.E89 2011
    658.3'1245—dc22

                                                              2010020923

About AMA
American Management Association (www.amanet.org) is a world leader in talent development, advancing the skills of individuals to drive business success. Our mission is to support the goals of individuals and organizations through a complete range of products and services, including classroom and virtual seminars, webcasts, webinars, podcasts, conferences, corporate and government solutions, business books, and research. AMA's approach to improving performance combines experiential learning—learning through doing—with opportunities for ongoing professional growth at every step of one's career journey.

Printing number
10 9 8 7 6 5 4 3 2

CONTENTS

PART I

PUTTING YOUR BEST FACE FORWARD

PART II

PUTTING YOUR CUSTOMERS FIRST

PART III

PUTTING IT ALL TOGETHER

ACKNOWLEDGMENTS

My deep appreciation to . . .

My editor, **Bob Nirkind**. Thank you! You illustrated what exceptional customer service is all about by listening well and by offering insightful, constructive suggestions and solutions that made me a better writer.

My copyeditor, **Barbara Chernow**. Thank you for paying attention to all the details, both small and large.

My agent, **Michael Snell**. Thank you for watching out for my best interests, for being my toughest critic, and for giving me advice that is always on target.

My husband and best friend, **Joseph Balka**. Thank you for always giving me great advice and ideas.

My mother, **Rose**. Thank you for being my extra eyes and catching the small details that I seem to miss.

My brother, **Don**. Thank you for lending your training expertise and giving me spot-on advice for the training tips sections.

My sister and training partner, **Sharon**. Thank you for always being there when I need an honest opinion.

My **clients**. Thank you for showing me how to give you the same level of customer service that I coach you to give your customers. I listen closely to what you want and then do my best to provide it to you.

My **family and friends**. Thank you for helping me be the best I can be every day.

I am deeply grateful for each and every one of you.

—Renée Evenson

Introduction

We are slowly coming out of the worst recession in more than a generation. It is estimated that millions of businesses closed their doors. Numerous others filed for bankruptcy protection. Experts acknowledge that recovery will be very slow, which means that more businesses are likely to close their doors.

With consumer confidence and customer loyalty at an all-time low, providing exceptional customer service is no longer an added benefit; it is a necessity. Customers who are not satisfied with the way they are treated are jumping ship and taking their business elsewhere. Customer loyalty can be your key to restoring consumer confidence, which can keep your business afloat. **Can you afford *not* to read this book?** Think about it this way: Giving your customers an exceptional experience will bring an unexpected result: your customers become a marketing tool for your business. Customers talk. When people hear good things about your business, they are more likely to do business with you as well.

Whether you are reading this book for the first time or already own the first edition, this new and improved version is your one-stop shop to learn and teach how to give exceptional customer service.

In addition to being thoroughly revised and updated throughout, this edition includes a new chapter:

- *Giving When Getting Is Not Expected: Self-Service Contacts* explains how to provide a great customer experience when your customers least expect it.

1

Moreover, each chapter has been expanded to include:

■ The wrong way/right way to handle contacts.

■ Tips and topics for brainstorming discussions.

■ A new feature, *Business NOT as Usual*, that provides ideas and tips for sustaining your business during tough times.

■ A revised *Practice Lesson*.

■ A new feature, *Doing It Right!*, that highlights a personal story.

■ A new feature, *How Do I Measure Up?*, that asks thought-provoking questions to help you analyze your skill level.

Every component of learning how to interact well with customers is included:

■ Displaying courtesy and respect by making a great first impression, speaking and acting appropriately, maintaining a positive attitude, and acting ethically.

■ Communicating well by saying what you mean to say, projecting proper body language, asking and answering questions correctly, and listening carefully.

■ Building strong relationships by establishing a rapport, interacting positively with customers, identifying needs, and finding the best solution.

■ Handling customers skillfully in face-to-face, telephone, Web site, and self-service settings.

■ Satisfying customers who are upset or difficult.

Customer service training benefits everyone involved. Your customers will feel valued and appreciated. Your employees will gain more job satisfaction, take personal responsibility for customers, and have pride in knowing they are doing their best. You will become more customer focused and seek out ways to continually improve. Your business will experience increased efficiency and effectiveness.

Can you afford **not** *to read this book?* The answer is simple: Providing great customer service costs much less, in dollars and sense, than providing poor service. It costs more to gain new customers than it does to maintain existing ones. Customers will be more loyal to your business when you treat them well. This book provides you with the tools to make the difference with your customers.

Finally, it is always cheaper and faster to do the job right the first time. Satisfying an unhappy customer costs a lot more, both in dollars and cents, than satisfying a customer on the first try. Reading this book will show you how to do that.

Tips for the Trainer

**TRAINING SESSIONS SHOULD
BE A POSITIVE EXPERIENCE
FOR BOTH THE TRAINER AND THE TRAINEE**

A trainer's most important role is to ensure that the frontline employees learn the fundamentals of providing exceptional customer service to every customer all the time. Investing the time to train your employees can be a fun and positive experience for both you and them.

Whether you are training your employees, your coworkers, a group of employees you were hired to train, or your students in school, thorough preparation will enable you to make the most out of your classes. Preparation before you begin will help you feel comfortable and confident and will take the guesswork out of your expectations. Preparation includes identifying your training needs, defining learning outcomes, planning your teaching lessons, establishing time frames for training sessions, preparing yourself for the training, setting up the room, and following up after the training.

IDENTIFY YOUR TRAINING NEEDS

To identify your training needs, answer this question: Why did you decide to conduct customer service training? Your immediate response might be "because we need it," but to answer this question reflectively you must first analyze and identify *what* needs to be improved from both your business and your employees' perspectives.

First, focus on your business. Make a list of your customer service training needs as they specifically relate to the type of products or services you provide, as well as your customers' needs. As you read through the book, relate the material to your business. For example, when reading the chapter on telephone contacts, you may have an "aha" moment and realize that your employees answer the phone in an unprofessional manner.

Next, focus on your employees' needs. Make a customer service learning outcome list for each employee. Note strengths, areas of improvement, additional technical or job skills training needed, and any behavioral issues (such as a poor attitude toward customers) that need to be addressed.

DEFINE LEARNING OUTCOMES

Review the needs you identified and develop a list of realistic learning outcomes. What skills should all of your employees demonstrate at the end of the training session? It might help to note each chapter title and make a list of the skills in which your employees should be proficient.

Using the example of employees answering calls in an unprofessional manner, one learning outcome for that chapter could be: Answer the telephone as ABC Company, then (employee's first name), then how may I help you? Listing specific outcomes before you begin training will enable you to measure how well your employees are using their new skills.

If you identified behavioral issues, you may want to make a separate list for those employees. This will help you focus on those items throughout the training sessions and follow up afterward.

PLAN YOUR TEACHING LESSONS

Create an introduction to kick off the training. Keep in mind that you will have everyone's undivided attention—during the first few minutes of speaking! Use this to your advantage and develop a strong introduction. Keep it short and stick to the basics. Explain why you are conducting this training and discuss general learning objectives. Then ask a question, tell a customer service story, or begin with a warm-up exercise or game. Make these first few minutes grab your students' attention. As you work through each chapter (those applicable), try this approach:

- Begin each chapter by relating a positive personal experience in which you were a customer (or ask for a student to volunteer) and _____ (fill in the blank to relate to the chapter material). For example, for Chapter 1, your example could be where you were a customer and formed a great first impression of an employee. Discuss the impact of the positive experience.

- Ask an open-ended question relevant to the example you cited. For example: *Why is it important to present yourself positively at all times?* Allow everyone to answer and discuss.

- Work through the material step by step. Vary your delivery by reading out loud to the students, having them take turns reading out loud, or reading to themselves.

- Throughout each chapter, ask discussion questions related specifically to your business. For instance, *What are some things we should do to make a positive first impression?*

- After reviewing each chapter, plan a group activity. Suggestions are:
  - Divide the group into teams. Assign a customer-related problem, dilemma, or question. Specify a time period for solving the problem. Each team will then present its solution to the group. Debate and choose the best solution.
  - Divide the group into role-play pairs. Give each pair a customer service scenario and some additional details to help them get into their roles. For example, the customer is upset with your company and the employee has a condescending attitude. Have one student play the role of the customer and another play the customer service employee. First have students role play the contact the wrong way, then again, role playing using the skills they are learning.
  - To energize the class, play a game related to the material. For example, after completing a session, have the group members close their books and call out the key points for the chapter they just completed. Toss a piece of candy to students as they answer correctly. Another option is to have a student call out an answer, then toss a ball to another person who must call out an answer.

- Review and recap the key points. Have students complete the Practice Lesson and discuss their answers.

- Have students complete *How Do I Measure Up?* Encourage them to honestly analyze their skill levels.

ESTABLISH TIME FRAMES FOR TRAINING SESSIONS

Now that you have reviewed the training material and planned your lessons, you should be able to establish time frames. Think about your hours of operation, busy periods, and employee coverage. It is most effective, and probably easiest, to cover the material in multiple sessions. This allows students to become comfortable with the material learned in each chapter.

When scheduling your classes, add a little extra time to your estimate to make sure your students will not feel rushed. Write a schedule to which you can conform. You will lose credibility with your employees if you schedule a class and then cancel. Give your training sessions top priority. If you demonstrate that customer service training is important to you, learning customer service skills will be important to your employees.

PREPARE YOURSELF FOR THE TRAINING

When you train, establish an open and relaxed atmosphere that encourages discussion by maintaining a positive attitude, keeping focused, remaining neutral, staying relaxed, encouraging everyone to participate, and focusing on goals.

Rehearse and practice your presentations—both the general introduction and how you plan to handle each chapter. It is perfectly normal to feel nervous, particularly if training is not part of your routine responsibilities. Being well prepared will help you manage your nerves. Practice may not make perfect, but it will help you gain confidence and feel more assured. Here are some tips for training others:

- Focus on your students rather than on yourself.

- Keep in mind the importance of the material.

- Stay on track by making good notes—and using them.

- Try to stick to the allotted time, but be sure you plan enough time to be thorough. Do not rush against a time clock. It is better to adjust the time than the material.

- When you speak, make eye contact with your students, switching your gaze from one person to another in a pace that is comfortable, not staged.

- Vary your voice tone and inflection.

- Be yourself. Act naturally.

- If you become nervous, take slow, deep breaths to calm yourself.

SET UP THE ROOM

Plan a setting conducive to training. First, find a suitable room or area that is free from distractions and noise. For a small group, a u-shaped, rectangular, or round table works well. This way the students can face each other for discussions, and you will be able to move easily within and around the group. If you will be using an easel or chalkboard for discussion answers, place it so that all students can see it.

Think of ways to energize your students. Look for signs of tiredness or boredom—yawning, fidgeting, or a glazed-over look. Here are some tips for energizing your group:

- Schedule short breaks every hour or two.

- Lead frequent stretching or deep breathing exercises.

- Vary the class activities.

- Keep the class interactive by leading frequent discussions and other activities.

FOLLOW UP AFTER THE TRAINING

Spend time with your employees to observe their customer contacts. Try to catch them "doing it right." When they do, acknowledge good performance by giving feedback that is specific to the behavior you observed.

Rather than saying, "you did a great job," be more specific by saying, "I really liked the way you handled Mrs. Johnson when she was upset. The way you explained our delivery schedule was right on target, and you made sure she understood completely. Great job." Now your employee knows exactly what was done right, and the behavior is more apt to be repeated.

It can be a great motivator to praise an employee in earshot of other employees, but it is never acceptable to discuss poor performance in public. When you hear an employee handling a customer poorly, take that employee aside to discuss the incident.

Recognize your group's efforts by commending them, by awarding total team efforts, and by reading customer commendations at meetings.

Most importantly, be consistent with your team. Recognizing good behavior yesterday but ignoring it today will confuse your employees. Make sure customer service is important to you every day; then it will be important to your employees every day, as well.

Tips for the Student

**WELL-TRAINED EMPLOYEES ARE
THE KEY TO SATISFIED CUSTOMERS**

Why is customer service training important? The answer is simple: treating your customers well is essential to your company and to your job. Learning how to give exceptional customer service is necessary for any business to succeed.

What can happen if customer service is not important to a business?

PICTURE THIS:...
THE WRONG WAY TO HANDLE CUSTOMERS

Kris began a new job working in a gift shop. She enjoyed stocking shelves and arranging merchandise in the display cases and window. She also got along well with her coworkers and manager, who joked around and had a good time. They even had an inside joke that it would be nice if customers did not bother them. When a customer came in, they would busy themselves with their "real work," ignoring the shopper until they were asked for help; they would then make jokes in the back room about who got stuck handling the customer.

After Kris had been working in the shop a few months, she noticed that fewer customers were coming in than when she first started. Business was dropping off. The employees enjoyed the relaxed atmosphere and had more time to joke around.

One day their manager held a meeting. She told the employees that their sales had been declining to the point that without sufficient sales revenue the company could not afford to keep all of them. Not long afterward, Kris and most of the other employees were let go.

Kris was upset. She liked working in the gift shop because it was so much fun. But she was upset for the wrong reason. Had it not been for the attitude she and her coworkers shared, the shop may not have lost business and have had to let employees go. Having fun on the job is fine, but Kris did not understand the most important rule of working in the customer service field: CUSTOMERS = REVENUE = WAGES = EMPLOYEES.

Customer service training is important because customers have many choices. If they are not happy with the way they are treated, they can take their business elsewhere, as did the customers in the scenario above.

> **Customers are the Reason You Have a Job!**

If Kris and her coworkers had been taught this simple principle, they would have treated their customers differently.

PICTURE THIS...
THE RIGHT WAY TO HANDLE CUSTOMERS

Kris began a new job working in a gift shop. On her first day, her manager trained Kris on her job duties, which included stocking shelves and arranging merchandise in the display cases and window. Her most important job, her manager stressed, was to help customers when they came in. No matter what Kris was doing, when a customer came in, she was to focus her attention on helping that customer. Her manager specifically explained the procedures and expectations for helping customers from the time they walked into the shop until the time they left.

Kris enjoyed stocking shelves and arranging merchandise in the display cases and window. She also got along well with her coworkers, who joked around and had a good time. When customers came in, they were given top priority, no matter what the employees were doing. Because the manager explained the importance of customers, Kris and her coworkers understood that helping customers was their most important job.

The manager held weekly group meetings. She kept the group up to date on sales revenue data, consistently discussed the importance of customer service, and praised exceptional behavior.

Kris enjoyed the relaxed atmosphere, where everyone worked to achieve the clearly stated company goals. Kris found tremendous job satisfaction helping customers in the gift shop.

Whether your manager purchased this book for a training class, you purchased this book to improve your skills, or you are using it for a class in school, you are going to learn how to present yourself well and how to handle different types of customers in varying situations.

Before you begin your training classes or reading the book, it will be beneficial to identify your personal needs and define learning outcomes. This will help you prepare for learning new skills, enable you to get the most out of the material, and help you self-monitor after training.

IDENTIFY YOUR PERSONAL NEEDS AND DEFINE LEARNING OUTCOMES

Think about your typical customer contacts. Which types of customers or customer interactions are you uncomfortable handling? For example, are you unsure how to talk to customers who are upset and confront you in an angry tone? Make a list of any areas in which you need improvement or guidance.

Now, think about your job from a technical standpoint. What must you learn to do your job effectively? Make a list of those areas in which you need additional training. Before you begin your customer service training, give this list to your manager and ask for the technical training you need. You must feel comfortable with your job duties before you can feel comfortable helping each customer.

Finally, think about what you want to gain from training. Make a list of learning outcomes. Turn your areas of improvement into learning outcomes by rephrasing them as positive statements. For example, not knowing how to deal with customers who are angry could be written as a learning objective: turn irate customers into satisfied ones.

PREPARE FOR THE TRAINING SESSION

Whether you are a student in a class or working through the material on your own, reading and learning puts you into a different routine. When you are used to working with customers and coworkers, staying alert when you sit, read, and work through a book can be difficult. Make the most of the training sessions by:

- Getting enough sleep the night before training.

- Eating a healthy breakfast.

- Knowing what to expect during the class.

- Taking deep breaths when you feel drowsy.

- Standing and stretching when you feel sleepy.

- Taking a short walking break when you feel ready to nod off.

GET THE MOST OUT OF THE MATERIAL

As you work through each chapter, relate what you are reading to the type of customer interactions you have. You may choose to focus on a specific customer scenario for each chapter. If you do, use the blank pages in Part II to write down a typical customer request. You can refer to this scenario when answering the Practice Lesson questions.

Each chapter follows a similar format:

- General chapter information

- "The Wrong Way To _____"

- Overview of the key points that will be covered in the chapter

- Next, each key point is explained step by step in an in-depth manner, followed by "The Right Way To _____." Note: In "The Right Way To," the same scenario is used several times within each chapter. Each scenario shows an outcome that builds on the steps presented in the chapter. The final "Picture This: Putting It All Together" recaps the scenario for the chapter, with the best approach to customer service.

- Business Not As Usual

- Summary of Key Points and Steps

- Practice Lesson

- Doing It Right!

- How Do I Measure Up?

In addition, each chapter contains handy tips and "Brainstorm" topics, which are designed for workgroup or classroom discussions.

If you are learning on your own, read through a chapter, then review the key points and steps. If you feel comfortable with the material, work the Practice Lesson. If you are not comfortable, go back over the chapter.

Make sure you understand the material before moving on. Give yourself time to practice the steps in each chapter before proceeding.

SELF-MONITOR AFTER TRAINING

Review your list of learning outcomes. Do you feel comfortable that you have mastered each? If not, review the relevant chapters again. Then, if you still feel uncomfortable or unsure, talk to your manager so together you can turn areas requiring improvement into strengths.

Most importantly, enjoy the work you do. Your customers and coworkers depend on you to be your best.

PART ONE

PUTTING YOUR BEST FACE FORWARD

1

Taking Your First Steps: The Basics

**ALWAYS REMEMBER, THE CUSTOMER
IS THE REASON YOU HAVE A JOB**

What has happened to customer service? More often than not, customers are met with boredom, indifference, and even rudeness or condescension. When they are greeted with a friendly smile, they are thrilled. When they are approached with a helpful attitude, they are likely to tell their friends. When they get good service, they are grateful. Customers should never have to feel grateful for being treated well. Being treated well should be the standard.

Think, for a moment, about your own interactions as a customer. In the past few days, how many times were you a customer? Did you go to the grocery store or the mall? Did you visit the post office, doctor's office, bank, dry cleaners, or your child's school? Did you eat any meals out? Did you call a company to ask a question or visit a Web site and order products online?

You probably were a customer more times then you realized. And as a customer, you have choices. How many stores are in your mall? How many doctors are in your phone book? How many restaurants are nearby? How easy is it to place an order by phone or online? If you are not happy with the service at one business, you have options. You can go elsewhere.

As a service provider, keep in mind that your customers have the same choices you do. If they are not happy with the way you treat them, they can go elsewhere.

How you treat your customers does matter. Think again about your own interactions as a customer. Which ones stand out in your mind? You are likely to remember service that is either outstanding or awful. Mediocre service is soon forgotten.

CUSTOMER SERVICE IS THE BASICS

We are going to take our first steps with the basics because:

The Basics Are the Basis of Customer Service.

A favorable first impression gets your customer service off on the right foot. You begin providing service the moment a customer comes into your business, calls you on the telephone, or e-mails you. When customers physically walk through your door, they take a mental snapshot of you and your surroundings. Without even thinking, they form a first impression. First impressions are also formed over the telephone and through online contact. How you speak, how well you listen, the words you choose, and how you write and respond using e-mail all contribute to first impressions. If a customer's first impression is favorable, you have laid the foundation for providing great customer service. If the first impression is not favorable, you will have to dig deeper to begin building your foundation.

Being courteous promotes a positive first impression. Customers appreciate courteous treatment. As young children, we learned basic courtesies: to say "please" and "thank you"; to pay attention and not to interrupt when other people speak; to treat others with respect; to play fairly; to say "I'm sorry." As adults, we sometimes forget how important these words and actions are. Courtesy words, phrases, and behaviors contain powerful messages. They show you care.

A positive attitude fosters a good first impression. Customers appreciate a positive attitude. A great attitude can help overcome a poor first impression. Similarly, a negative attitude can destroy a favorable first impression.

Being truthful and acting in an ethical manner completes the picture of the first impressions you make. Honesty is always the best policy. When you follow through on commitments and stay accountable for your actions, you show your customers that you value them and that they can rely on you to do the right thing.

By combining a favorable first impression, courteous treatment, a positive attitude, and ethical behaviors, you form the basis for a strong customer service foundation. Add effective communication skills, and you will be on your way to building long-lasting relationships with your customers. Once you master these customer service basics, learn how to effectively communicate, and develop skills to build strong relationships, you will confidently handle any customer in any situation.

PICTURE THIS...
THE WRONG WAY TO PROVIDE BASIC SERVICE

Sally drove to Bob's Electronics store to look for a new television set. She walked in and spotted two employees stocking DVD players on a display rack. They were laughing and joking with each other as they worked. Neither looked at her. Neither asked if she needed help. She asked if they carry television sets. Without looking up, one of the employees said, "Yeah, they're over there," pointing as he answered. She wandered over to the television sets. With so many new types from which to choose, she was confused and did not know what she wanted. She noticed the employees were still joking around. Sally waited a few moments and when neither one paid attention to her, she walked out of the store.

What Went Wrong?

Sally did not form a favorable first impression of the employees at Bob's Electronics Store. Neither stopped what they were doing to help her. Neither was courteous. They could have changed her first impression by projecting an attitude that they cared about her as a customer and by taking the time to help her.

How Did the Customer Feel?

Sally was dissatisfied with the way she was treated. It appeared to her that the employees considered stocking shelves and talking to each other were more important than helping her. Sally felt that her business simply did not matter to Bob's employees. Since she did not care for the way she was treated, Sally left without doing business with them.

When you work with customers continuously, it is easy to begin taking them for granted, but taking customers for granted is never acceptable. When you do, you stop caring about how you treat them. Eventually, you may view customers as intruders who take you away from your work. This was the view Bob's employees projected. To them, stocking shelves and talking to each other were more important. If you do not treat your customers well, you may soon have no customers.

Customers, on the other hand, have been conditioned to expect mediocre service. Customers who are given mediocre service will have mediocre attitudes about the business. When customers are valued and treated with courtesy and respect, they are more apt to do repeat business with you. Remember the important lesson you learned as a child: Always treat others the way you want to be treated. Treat others well, and they are more likely to treat you well.

Mastering the basics is simple once you learn and practice the four steps below. Then you will begin to build a firm foundation for providing great customer service.

Step 1: First Impressions Matter

Step 2: Courtesy Counts

Step 3: Attitude Is Everything

Step 4: Doing the Right Thing: Ethical Issues

If Bob's employees treated Sally better, she would not have walked out of the store. She left because they did not value her as a customer. They did not lay a foundation for giving great customer service.

STEP 1
FIRST IMPRESSIONS MATTER

First impressions are mental snapshots you take when you first encounter a person or situation. They include a person's looks and actions: general grooming and cleanliness, clothing, tone of voice, attitude, body language, and posture. Together, these elements make up an individual's personal style. First impressions do matter. They matter a lot.

When Sally took her mental snapshot at Bob's, it did not develop well. Even if the employees were well dressed, had neat hair, and wore clean clothes, their lack of courtesy and poor attitudes spoke volumes. When they ignored Sally, they told her loudly and clearly that they did not value her as a customer.

Appearance Is the First Thing Customers Notice About You

The first step to making a good first impression is your appearance. An unappealing appearance can be an obstacle that blocks customers from forming a positive first impression. You may have to sacrifice your personal style to please others, but your appearance at work needs to fit your business. Otherwise, you may have to work harder for your customers to become comfortable with you.

Wear Appropriate Clothing for the Type of Work You Do

Wear the type of clothing that fits the character of your business. If you work in a five-star restaurant, you will dress quite differently than if you work in a fast food restaurant. When in doubt, always lean toward dressing conservatively. Save your party clothes for parties. Save your torn jeans and old tees for hanging out with friends. No matter what type of clothes you wear to work, you do not have to spend a fortune on your wardrobe. Wearing well-fitted and appropriate clothes will go a long way toward presenting yourself successfully. It does not matter how much you spend; what matters most is how your clothes fit you and your environment.

Make Sure You Are Groomed

Being groomed means your hair and fingernails are clean and neat; your face, body, and teeth are clean; your clothes are clean and pressed; your shoes are polished; your hair is styled; and your overall image is professional. Put all that together, and you present a groomed look.

TIP

If you do not have a full-length mirror, buy one. Look in it every day before you leave home.

Maintain a Relaxed and Open Demeanor

You can wear nice clothes, be clean and groomed, yet still convey a negative first impression. Your body language counts as much as your grooming. Whether you present an angry, bored, or friendly demeanor, it shows. Hold your head high, and keep your facial expressions friendly. Make eye contact when talking with someone. And smile as often as appropriate. A smile goes a long way in establishing a good interpersonal relationship. When you smile, you feel better. When you smile, you make others feel better.

Doing these three things will help your customers form a positive first impression of you. Doing these three things shows that you care about yourself.

PICTURE THIS...
THE RIGHT WAY TO MAKE A GREAT FIRST IMPRESSION

Sally drove to Bob's Electronics Store to purchase a new television set. She walked in and spotted two employees stocking DVDs on a display rack. They were dressed nicely and looked happy, laughing and joking with each other while they worked. They looked at her, smiled, and said, "Welcome to Bob's." The employees were well groomed, and their body language conveyed the message that they cared about themselves. Their smiles conveyed the message that they cared about her. Sally smiled back and said she was looking for a new television.

How Did the Customer Feel?

This time Sally's mental snapshot was developing nicely. The employees made a great first impression because they stopped what they were doing to greet her.

STEP 2
COURTESY COUNTS

Young children are praised for doing and saying the right things. When a young child says "please" and "thank you," people respond positively. When a young child says "I'm sorry," people readily accept the apology. When children wait to speak without interrupting, people notice how well mannered they are. When children learn how to play well, people comment. Children who receive positive reinforcement develop valuable skills for getting along with others.

As an adult, you are not going to receive constant praise for being courteous, but people will appreciate these behaviors. When you act courteously, you send a positive and powerful message. When you make a conscious effort to use courtesy words and phrases, they will soon become a natural part of your vocabulary and personality.

Say Please, Thank You, and You're Welcome

We were taught these words as young children, and they were reinforced frequently. Do you remember being prompted, "What do you say?" Do you remember responding with "please" or "thank you" or "you're welcome"? Pay attention to your internal prompts. Make it a habit to incorporate these words into your vocabulary and use them frequently.

Say Excuse Me and I'm Sorry

Growing up, you learned that when you did not understand someone, when someone was in your way, or when you inadvertently did something incorrectly, you said "excuse me." When you did something wrong or made a mistake you learned to say "I'm sorry." Saying "I'm sorry" can be particularly difficult for adults. Get in the habit of adding this to your vocabulary. The next time you do something wrong, say "I'm sorry." Not only will you make the other person feel better, you will feel better. These two words go a long way in repairing relationship damage.

Use Sir and Ma'am

Using these words shows a sign of respect. When you call a person sir or ma'am, be careful how you accentuate these words. The wrong emphasis can make you sound sarcastic or condescending. The right emphasis can make you sound respectful, no matter your age or your customer's age.

Use a Person's Name When You Know It

Everyone enjoys hearing his or her name, so if you know your customer's name, use it. Also be sure to give the customer your name.

Use Yes Rather Than Yeah

"Yes" sounds professional, intelligent, and respectful. Period. Save "yeah" for personal conversations. Better yet, get into the habit of always using "yes."

Say It with a Smile

This is an old saying with a timely meaning. In our speed-of-light-paced world, smiling when you speak does come across loud and clear. Whether you are speaking face to face or by telephone, your customers will see or hear the smile in your voice.

TIP

Common courtesies include things you should not do in the presence of customers, including talking on a personal call, smoking, eating (or having food at your work station), and chewing gum.

PICTURE THIS...
THE RIGHT WAY TO INCORPORATE BASIC COURTESIES

Sally smiled back at the two employees and said, "I'm looking for a new television, but there are so many new types I really don't know what I'm looking for. Can you help me?"

"Yes ma'am. My name is Jeff, and I'll be happy to help you," said one of the employees as he smiled warmly and walked toward her. "Let me show you what we have." He walked with her to the television sets.

How Did the Customer Feel?
Jeff was courteous and Sally felt that he truly cared about helping her.

ATTITUDE IS EVERYTHING

People may not remember the color of the shirt you wore or the exact words you said, but they will remember your attitude. Projecting a positive attitude is another way to make a good—and long-lasting—impression on others. It really is all in the presentation. The "IT" factor is the attitude you present to the world.

Attitude Is Everything

Good or bad. Whether your attitude is good or bad, it is what people are going to remember about you. Remember that you may not get a second chance to interact with customers. Even if you are not a naturally upbeat person, you can train yourself to have a more positive attitude. It begins by learning to appreciate.

Appreciate the Good in Yourself and in Others

Appreciation can be learned by changing your self-talk (the words you use when you think) to positive thoughts. This goes for thoughts about yourself as well: Change "I'll never do this right" to "Next time I'll do better." This also goes for thoughts about your customers: "Look at this old lady. She doesn't look like she has a clue about television sets. She is going to be tough to deal with." Change this mindset to: "I'll do what I can to help this customer. She mentioned she doesn't know a whole lot about all the new type sets, so I'll do my best to explain them all." Changing your self-talk helps you appreciate yourself and others. When you find yourself falling into old habits of negative self-talk, make a conscious effort to change your thought process.

Believe in Yourself

When you stop your negative self-talk, you will start to believe in yourself. Saying things such as "I'll never do this right" only sets you up for failure. Changing your self-talk to "Next time I'll do it differently" sets you up for success. When you begin to believe in yourself, you will begin to feel more confident. When you feel more confident, you will begin projecting a powerful image to others. To your customers, you will project an image of someone who believes in yourself, your company, and your products.

Believe You Can Make a Difference

When you believe in yourself and gain confidence, you will naturally progress to believing that you can make a difference in the lives of others. When you believe you can make a difference, you will find ways to make it happen. At work, look for ways to make a difference by being helpful, interested, and caring toward your customers.

Keep an Open Mind; Do Not Stereotype People

When the employee thought about the older woman who did not know what she wanted and was going to be tough to deal with, he was accepting a negative stereotype about older people before he even talked to her. That older woman could surprise him. Remember first impressions? Stereotypes can skew first impressions. Do you want people to stereotype you? When you change your thought process and stop stereotyping others, you will change the way you present yourself.

Maintain Your Positive Attitude

Negative circumstances can easily zap anyone's positive attitude. If someone has upset you, or if you find yourself feeling stressed, try to get away from the situation for a few minutes. Getting away will not only help you calm down, it will give you time to think through the situation and put things in perspective. The best remedy for maintaining a positive attitude is to take care of you every day. Get enough rest. Exercise your body and mind. Eat healthy foods. Do something fun. Do something just for you. When you do these things every day, you will find it easier to stay upbeat and positive.

TIP

> We all carry emotional baggage. When you arrive at work, leave your emotional baggage at the door. Never make your customers and coworkers suffer because you are having a problem. Remember that everyone has problems. Use your work time to put aside your personal baggage.

PICTURE THIS...
THE RIGHT WAY TO DISPLAY A POSITIVE ATTITUDE

As they walked to the television sets, Jeff asked, "Have you been to Bob's before?" When Sally shook her head, he smiled and continued enthusiastically, "I'm glad you came in. Not only do we offer the lowest prices around, we stand behind all our merchandise."

Sally nodded. She liked what she was hearing.

When they reached the television display, Jeff said, "I'll tell you about the different types of sets we have and be happy to answer any questions." He took the time to answer all her questions and guided her to make the right choice.

How Did the Customer Feel?

Sally completed developing her mental snapshot. Because she liked Jeff's confident, positive attitude, Sally trusted him to give her good suggestions.

STEP 4
DOING THE RIGHT THING: ETHICAL ISSUES

The last step of customer service basics deals with ethics. Being ethical means being honest, doing the right thing, and being accountable for your actions.

Always Be Honest

Being honest at all times will make your life far less complicated. When you are truthful, you do not have to remember what you said to whom. Being truthful is important to your customers. When you are dishonest, people find out. Maybe not right away, but the truth always has a way of coming out. When people find out you have not been completely honest, they will no longer trust you.

Always Be Truthful About Your Products, Services, and Policies

Never make misleading claims or comment negatively about your competitors. If a customer asks for a comparison or leads you to say something negative, say, "I don't know about that but let me explain our policy. . . ." or "I don't know enough about that to comment."

Do the Right Thing

When you make the decision to always do the right thing for others, you will go out of your way to do your best. At work, when you are faced with a dilemma, base your decision on doing what is right and ethical. Being ethical includes treating all your customers fairly and equally.

Do What You Say You Will When You Say You Will

Become a person others can rely on. When you give a customer your word, mean it. Let your word be your bond. Erase the words "I can't" and "no" from your vocabulary. If you cannot do what the customer asks, explain instead what you can do. It is all right to say "I don't know." Follow up with "I'll find out for you."

Stay Accountable for Your Actions

If you think you have done something incorrect or unethical, be upfront and talk it over with your manager. When you take responsibility and own up to your mistakes, people will respect you. No one expects you to make the right decision 100 percent of the time. We are all human and are all going to make mistakes. What sets ethical people apart is that they hold themselves accountable for their mistakes. This may not be easy at first, but it is the right thing to do. People will appreciate that you are able to admit you did something wrong. You will also have an added benefit: You will respect yourself more when you take responsibility for your actions.

PICTURE THIS...
THE RIGHT WAY TO HANDLE AN ETHICAL ISSUE

Sally was ready to buy. She said, "I heard that JB Appliances gives four free DVDs when you purchase a television. I'll buy from you if you give me some DVDs."

Jeff was not familiar with JB's policy. Before he answered, he thought about what to say. He could have said, "JB offers that because the store sells its televisions at a higher price and doesn't stand behind its merchandise. I've heard complaints about the store." Or he might have said, "Well, we usually don't do that, but for you I'll make an exception."

Here is how Jeff answered Sally: "I'm not familiar with what JB Appliances offers, but here's what we offer. We keep our merchandise priced low to consistently give our customers the best deal. And we stand behind our products."

By positively reassuring Sally and explaining their policy, Jeff did not get involved in an ethical dilemma. Sally left Bob's with a new television set.

How Did the Customer Feel?

Sally bought her television set at Bob's because she felt that Jeff's honest and ethical response was more important than some free DVDs.

Do you know what is ethical, and more importantly, unethical, in your business? If you are unclear, discuss specific situations that may be considered unethical with your manager or instructor. In today's business climate, every employee should be absolutely certain they know the difference. Even when you do understand your ethics policies, you may mishandle a situation. Let's say that one of your customers asks you to do something special or unusual, such as waiving a service fee. You willingly comply, but later realize that you crossed ethical boundaries. How do you handle the situation? Do you call the customer and retract the favor? Do you extend the favor to all customers, having done it for one?

Together with your workgroup or class, discuss how to handle sticky situations you may encounter. Then, come up with suggested responses. Role play to reinforce ethical behavior.

PICTURE THIS...
PUTTING IT ALL TOGETHER

Sally drove to Bob's Electronics Store to purchase a new television set. She walked in and spotted two employees stocking DVDs on a display rack. They were dressed nicely and looked happy, as they laughed and joked with each other while they worked. They looked at her, smiled, and said, "Welcome to Bob's." The employees were well groomed, and their body language conveyed the message that they cared about themselves. Their smiles conveyed the message that they cared about her.

Sally smiled back and said, "I'm looking for a new television, but there are so many new types I really don't know what I'm looking for. Can you help me?"

"Yes ma'am. My name is Jeff, and I'll be happy to help you," said one of the employees as he smiled warmly and walked toward her. "Let me show you what we have." He walked with her to the television sets.

Jeff asked, "Have you been to Bob's before?" When Sally shook her head, he smiled and continued enthusiastically, "I'm glad you came in. Not only do we offer the lowest prices around, we stand behind all our merchandise."

Sally nodded. She liked what she was hearing.

When they reached the television display, Jeff said, "I'll tell you about the different types of sets we have and be happy to answer any questions." He took the time to answer all her questions and guided her to make the right choice.

Sally was ready to buy. She said, "I heard that JB Appliances gives four free DVDs when you purchase a television. I'll buy from you if you give me some DVDs."

Jeff answered, "I'm not familiar with what JB Appliances offers, but here's what we offer. We keep our merchandise priced low to consistently give our customers the best deal. And we stand behind our products."

By positively reassuring Sally and explaining their policy, Jeff did not get involved in an ethical dilemma. Sally left Bob's with a new television set.

Customer service begins when you take the first steps by making a great first impression, being courteous, displaying a positive attitude, and being truthful and ethical with your customers. It really is that simple.

**BUSINESS
NØT
AS USUAL**

Always Remember: The Customer Is the Reason You Have a Job
Think about the truth in these words. It is always important to appreciate your customers, but when business takes a downturn, showing your appreciation to each and every one of your customers takes on a more important, literal meaning. Each customer who comes into your business may well be the one responsible for your job. So:

- Be helpful and enthusiastic.

- Keep your facial expressions friendly.

- Say it with a smile.

- Do everything with integrity.

- Never give the customer a reason to lose trust in your company.

- Attitude is everything—make sure yours is positive.

KEY POINTS

Step 1: First Impressions Matter

- Appearance is the first thing people notice about you.
- Wear appropriate clothing for the type of work you do.
- Make sure you are well groomed.
- Maintain a relaxed and open demeanor.

Step 2: Courtesy Counts

- Say "please," "thank you," and "you're welcome."
- Say "excuse me" and "I'm sorry."
- Use "sir" and "ma'am."
- Use a person's name when you know it.
- Use "yes" rather than "yeah."
- Say it with a smile.

Step 3: Attitude Is Everything

- Attitude is everything—good or bad.
- Appreciate the good in yourself and in others.
- Believe in yourself.
- Believe you can make a difference.
- Keep an open mind; do not stereotype people.

Step 4: Doing the Right Thing: Ethical Issues

- Always be honest.
- Do the right thing.
- Do what you say you will when you say you will.
- Stay accountable for your actions.

PRACTICE LESSON

Step 1: First Impressions Matter

Write down some things you can do to make a good first impression.

_____

_____

Step 2: Courtesy Counts

Write some statements you can say to your customers that incorporate basic courtesies.

_____

_____

_____

Step 3: Attitude Is Everything

What are some things you can do to present a great attitude?

_____

_____

_____

Step 4: Doing the Right Thing: Ethical Issues

Think of a situation in which a customer asks you to do something unethical. Briefly describe the situation and your response to the customer.

_____

_____

_____

D O I N G   I T   R I G H T !

John works part time in a tire store. He is attending technical college, training to be an auto technician. He hopes to one day own a repair shop. To some, his current position would be "just a job," a stepping stone to a better career. Yet, even though John earns little more than minimum wage, he treats this job as though it is the best job in the world. Every day he gives his customers, his boss, and his coworkers his all.

I was fortunate to walk into this tire store on a day when John was working. He looked directly at me, smiled, and greeted me warmly. "Hi, welcome to Westview Tire," he called out enthusiastically. "How can I help you today?" His "take charge" demeanor and outgoing personality told me loud and clear that I mattered. Upon meeting him, he made me feel like I was the most important person in the world. Even though I don't know a lot about tires, I knew I was in good hands.

After making a great first impression, I noticed that John frequently incorporated courtesy words and phrases into his vocabulary. He respectfully answered, "Yes ma'am," or "No ma'am." His upbeat attitude was refreshing.

His enthusiasm was contagious and I couldn't help but smile as he fully explained the different tires he had in stock, describing the pros and cons of each. My mental snapshot was developing nicely. He was knowledgeable and made sure he answered my questions thoroughly. Here is this guy, a student working part time in a tire store earning not much more than minimum wage, displaying more zest for his tires than most people do for their most valued possessions.

I complimented John to his boss, who smiled broadly. He told me how lucky he is to have hired John, commenting that "John's friendliness and his direct, honest approach usually develops into long-lasting relationships."

I asked John how he manages to stay so positive and upbeat everyday. His answer was great. "I appreciate this job, my boss, and my customers. I try to treat everyone the way I want to be treated."

When commenting on his ability to make a great first impression, John replied, "I always try my best to make a good first impression. After all, you never know who you're impressing!"

True words!

H O W   D O   I   M E A S U R E   U P ?

1. What first impression am I making with my customers?

   _____

   _____

2. What courtesy words and phrases am I remembering to use? Which ones do I need to remember to use?

   _____

   _____

3. How well am I maintaining a positive attitude? What are my "negative" triggers and what can I do to stay upbeat and positive?

   _____

   _____

4. How honest and ethical am I? Am I doing the right thing in all situations? If not, what can I do to correct these behaviors?

   _____

   _____

5. What can I do to be more like John?

   _____

   _____

2

Tossing the Ball Back and Forth: Effective Communication

**IN YOUR DEALINGS WITH CUSTOMERS,
BE THE ONE TO INITIATE HONEST, RESPECTFUL,
AND THOUGHTFUL COMMUNICATION**

Did you know that almost everything you do in life involves some form of communication? Anytime you interact with another person, you communicate. Whether you smile at a stranger, speak to a friend, or listen attentively when someone is talking to you, you communicate. You can even communicate by doing nothing at all. When you ignore someone, let a door close on the person behind you, or look the other way when someone is approaching, you communicate.

We communicate for numerous reasons. We communicate when we need to make decisions, solve problems, get answers, gather information, or resolve conflicts. We communicate when we want to find out how someone is doing, learn about something, discuss important events, or get to know someone. A smile communicates volumes. So does a scowl. Communicating is so important that a person's success often depends on good communication skills.

CUSTOMER SERVICE IS EFFECTIVE COMMUNICATION

As a front-line employee, you are your customers' point of contact and their primary source of communication. To them, you not only represent the company, you are the company.

As your company's communicator, how you communicate with your customers is important. In fact, it is your most important job. Relationships develop when effective communication is established. You will learn about building relationships in Chapter 3, but first you need to learn valuable communication skills. Communication forms the basis of any relationship; at work, learning how to communicate effectively is imperative when you deal with customers.

The easiest way to communicate is when you are face to face with people. You have the advantage of picking up cues about a person's moods and can adjust your conversation accordingly. You also communicate by telephone and by sending e-mails and letters. When you write, you have the advantage of being able to read—and change—your message before sending it. When speaking face to face, you have no backspace or delete key to change your message. It is crucial in verbal communication that you say exactly what you mean to say. Using good grammar helps communicate the correct message.

Try this verbal communication exercise: Ask the following question out loud in an enthusiastic tone:

"Can I help you?"

Now repeat it in:

An unsure tone.

A condescending tone.

A disinterested tone.

Notice how the same four words take on four very different meanings, depending on your tone of voice. *How* you say something is even more important than the words you choose. How you say something can help—or hinder—the effectiveness of your communication.

In addition to verbal communication, you can communicate without saying a word. When communicating face to face, an example is your body language, which is a major form of communication. Nonverbal communication, including your posture, facial expressions, and hand and eye movements, are all ways of communicating. You may say one thing but communicate something else. Words communicate a message; body language communicates the emotions behind the message.

Try this nonverbal communication exercise: Picture yourself explaining a company policy to a customer. As you are speaking:

Look at the person and smile.

Slump over and yawn.

Lower your eyes to the floor.

Stand with your arms folded in front of you.

When you look directly at someone and smile, you show interest. When you slump and yawn, you convey boredom. When you lower your eyes to the floor, you express disinterest or dishonesty. When you stand with your arms folded in front of you, you build an imaginary wall between you and the other person. You can say the right words, but still convey the wrong message.

As your company's communicator, it is important that what you say is interpreted the way you mean it. How many times has someone misunderstood your message? When that happens, it takes time and energy to correct the listener's interpretation. When you speak, choose your words carefully. When you listen, pay attention to what you hear.

A large part of your communication with customers is asking questions. Knowing what questions to ask is crucial, but so is knowing when to ask them. The tone you use when you ask a question is as important as the words you choose.

When you ask questions to find the right solutions, you may receive objections to your proposals. Learning how to handle objections is crucial to providing great customer service.

However, listening carefully may be considered the most important component in effective communication. Unless you listen completely, you may respond incorrectly or improperly. Listening carefully includes paying attention to what the customer is saying and to the customer's body language to ensure that you understand their emotions.

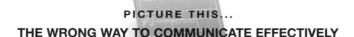

PICTURE THIS...
THE WRONG WAY TO COMMUNICATE EFFECTIVELY

Steve stopped at the local deli for lunch. He was in a hurry to place the order for himself and his coworkers and was greeted by an employee who yawned as he looked at Steve. Scratching his head with his pencil, he said, "Hey man, whaddyawant?"

"I'm in a hurry. Is it possible to get my order quickly?"

The employee shrugged nonchalantly. "I suppose so. We're not that busy right now."

Steve began to give his order, "I'll have a turkey and Swiss on whole wheat with mayo and tomatoes. . . ." As he spoke he noticed the employee kept looking at the door whenever someone came in. Steve finished his order, "a ham on rye with mustard and a pastrami on rye with mustard."

The employee said, "OK, a ham on rye and a pastrami on rye. What do you want on 'em?"

As Steve answered "mustard" he wondered if the employee got the rest of the order. "Did you get the turkey and Swiss, the roast beef, and the tuna salad?"

Without looking up, he said "Yeah" in an agitated voice. The employee strolled slowly to the backroom with Steve's order.

Before Steve left, he checked his order because he was not certain the employee got it right.

What Went Wrong?

The employee looked tired, bored, and was more interested in seeing who was coming in than helping Steve. His lack of attention, poor choice of words, and lazy grammar did nothing to help Steve feel confident that the order would be right.

How Did the Customer Feel?

Because the employee paid more attention to who was coming and going, Steve had no confidence that the employee got the order correct. He felt that the employee did not care about him as a customer and that the owner/manager did not care about the way the deli's employees handled customers.

Whether you work in a physician's office, a restaurant, a retail store, a professional office, a service station, or a call center, effective communication is always important. When your primary job is to be your company's communicator, you project your company's image to the customers. By learning the six steps that follow, you will learn valuable tools to help you become a more effective communicator.

Step 1: Saying What You Mean and Meaning What You Say

Step 2: What You Don't Say: Nonverbal Communication

Step 3: Putting Words Together: Grammar Usage

Step 4: Asking the Correct Questions and Answering the Questions Correctly

Step 5: When the Customer Says No

Step 6: Listening Actively

If the deli employee had communicated more effectively, Steve would have had more confidence that his order was correct. Although he was in a hurry to get back to his office, he took the time to check his order before leaving the deli.

STEP 1

SAYING WHAT YOU MEAN AND MEANING WHAT YOU SAY

When you communicate, you can either speak or listen. It is impossible to do both well at the same time. As the speaker, you control the conversation. You have the listener's attention—as long as you are saying something that interests your listener. As the speaker, it is your responsibility to get your message across the way you mean it. You may not get a second chance to explain.

Choose the Right Words

Think before you speak. Choose words that the listener will understand. When you speak to a customer who may not be familiar with your company or products, choose words that will convey the correct message. Opt for easy and familiar words. Trying to impress people with big words may only add confusion to your message.

Make Sure Your Tone Fits the Message You Are Sending

How you say something can be more important than what you say. When you did the verbal exercise on pages 42–43 and asked a question four different ways, you conveyed four different attitudes. In addition to choosing the right words, think about how you want to say them. When you talk to someone and use the wrong tone, your message may be misinterpreted. When speaking to a customer who is upset, use a serious, helpful tone. When asking a customer if you can help, use an enthusiastic tone. When asking a question, use a tone that shows you are truly interested in the answer. Pay attention to your listener's nonverbal cues to make sure your tone fits your customer.

Add Welcome Words to Your Vocabulary

When you use words that sound positive and confident, you will project a positive and confident attitude. Words and phrases such as "Yes!," "I'll be happy to!," and "Sure I can!" send the message that you are really happy to help your customers. Words such as "definitely" and "absolutely" send the message that you are enthusiastic and interested. It is difficult to say "definitely" without showing conviction and interest. It is difficult to say "absolutely" without showing enthusiasm. Interjecting these and other welcome words into your conversation adds a sense of conviction that you truly want to help.

Keep Business Conversations Professional

When you interact with customers, draw the line between being professional and getting personal. Even though you may establish a friendly rapport, your customer is still your customer. Keep these conversations on a professional level.

TIP

When you are speaking with a customer from a different culture for whom English is not a first language use the same tone and voice level you normally use, but choose different words. In fact, try to use fewer words to convey your message. Repeating the same misunderstood words over and over will most likely frustrate the customer—and you.

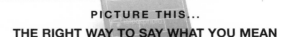

PICTURE THIS...
THE RIGHT WAY TO SAY WHAT YOU MEAN

Steve stopped at the local deli for lunch. He was in a hurry to place the order for himself and his coworkers and was greeted by an employee who looked at him, smiled, and enthusiastically said, "Hi, welcome to Max's Deli. How are you doing?"

"I'm doing great, thanks, but I'm in a hurry. Is it possible to get my order quickly?"

"Yes, absolutely. I'll put a rush on it. What can I get you?"

How Did the Customer Feel?

This time, the employee chose words that were appropriate and his tone of voice conveyed enthusiasm. Steve felt comfortable with the employee, and when the employee added "absolutely," Steve felt confident that he meant what he said.

STEP 2
WHAT YOU DON'T SAY: NONVERBAL COMMUNICATION

As already mentioned, how you say something can be more important than the words you choose. But your appearance and behavior when you send a message are also important. You can choose the right words and use an appropriate tone, but send an entirely different message through nonverbal communication. In the nonverbal exercise on page 43, you used four different approaches when you spoke to your customer. You said one thing, but sent four entirely different messages.

Remember That Actions Speak Louder Than Words

You may have a great attitude and personality, but your actions will leave a lasting impression on your customers. Always be aware of your body language to make sure you are sending the right nonverbal messages.

Smile Often

A smile is one of the most powerful messages you can send. A smile translates into any language, to any age group, across any culture. Smile and people will smile back at you. Try it. It does work. Get in the habit of smiling often. When you make it a habit to smile, your smile will look natural, not forced. A forced smile looks phony; sometimes a forced smile looks frozen on your face. When you smile often, your smile will become a natural part of your demeanor.

Keep a pleasant facial appearance by training your mouth muscles to turn slightly upward at the corners when you are in a relaxed pose.

Make Eye Contact

Eye contact is one of the most important components of communication, yet it can be a tough habit to get into. If you are uncomfortable making eye contact when you speak, first try to get into the habit of making eye contact when you listen. Nod, smile, and stay interested. When you are comfortable doing that, make a conscious effort to look at the other person when you speak. When your eyes stray, bring your focus back. Wandering eyes send a message that you are bored or more interested in someone or something other than the person you are with. Making eye contact is a powerful tool. Eye contact shows you are interested, honest, and confident.

Maintain a Relaxed, Open Demeanor

Maintaining good posture sends the message that you are confident. When standing, hold your head high, stand straight, and allow your arms to fall naturally at your sides with your hands relaxed and open. When seated, maintain good posture by sitting up straight. If you need to cross your legs, do so at the ankles and fold your hands in your lap if seated away from your desk. When gesturing with your hands, allow your gestures to flow naturally. If they are too exaggerated, people will focus more on your movements than on what you are saying.

TIP

> Try this posture exercise: Pretend you have a string attached to the top of your head. Imagine the string is being pulled straight up until you are standing tall and holding your head in a comfortable position. When you find yourself slumping, do the string exercise.

Keep Your Energy Level Steady

Choose healthy, nutritious foods that will give you long-lasting energy. If you start feeling drowsy at work, breathe deeply and do a few stretches. These can even be done inconspicuously at your desk or work station. Maintaining good posture also helps keep your energy level up. It is really tough to operate effectively when you are tired, so try your best to get enough rest. When you are well rested, you will think clearly, make sound decisions, care about the way you look, have patience, and stay attentive.

PICTURE THIS...
THE RIGHT WAY TO COMMUNICATE NONVERBALLY

Steve began to give his order: "I'll have a turkey and Swiss on whole wheat with mayo and tomatoes. . . ." As he spoke, he noticed that the employee looked directly at him before writing down the item. He smiled often, his demeanor told Steve he was interested, and he nodded occasionally as Steve spoke.

How Did the Customer Feel?
This time, the employee sent a message to Steve that he was interested in him as a customer. Steve felt relaxed as he waited for his order.

STEP 3
PUTTING WORDS TOGETHER: GRAMMAR USAGE

Proper grammar is critical to effective communication. When you use proper grammar, it is easier to send the right message. Save the "Hey man" and "Whaddyawant" for your friends.

Reflect Your Company's Personality

At work, you are the voice for your business, and you should always choose words that reflect your company's personality. In a deli setting, that personality will be fairly casual. In a white linen restaurant, it will be more formal. If you are unclear how you should speak to customers, how friendly or casual you should be, ask your manager for guidance.

Speak Clearly

Using overly casual terms or running words together can make a message difficult for some people to understand. Get in the habit of always using words in their correct form. Say "Hello" or "Hi" in place of "Hey man." Say "What would you like to order?" or "What can I get you?" in place of "Whaddyawant?" Speak clearly, and you will present yourself as an intelligent, competent person.

Use Everyday Language

In Step 1, you learned that choosing the right words helps you send the right message to your listener. When you have a choice between two words, always opt for the simpler and shorter of the two. Such words are easy for everyone to understand and you avoid the risk of sending the wrong message.

Avoid Using Slang, Jargon,
Company Terms, and Technical Language

Your customers are not likely to know company terms, acronyms, and jargon, so stick to common and generic words. Most customers will not understand technical terms, so when you need to give technical explanations, convert difficult-to-understand words into words to which your customer will relate. Always speak the language that your customers will understand. Try to match your speech to each customer's level of comprehension.

PICTURE THIS...
THE RIGHT WAY TO INCORPORATE PROPER GRAMMAR

The employee greeted Steve by saying, "Hi, welcome to Max's Deli. How are you doing?"

When it was time to take the order, he responded to Steve's statement about being in a hurry with, "Yes, absolutely. I'll put a rush on it. What can I get you?"

How Did the Customer Feel?

Steve appreciated that the employee used proper grammar and was clear in his speech.

STEP 4
ASKING THE CORRECT QUESTIONS AND ANSWERING THE QUESTIONS CORRECTLY

We ask questions for many reasons. As customers, we ask questions to gather information. Typically, employees ask questions to complete an order, solve a customer's problem, or resolve a customer's complaint.

The two types of questions are open and closed. Open questions require more than a yes or no answer and encourage the responder to provide information. Closed questions require only a one-word or short answer and are often used for clarification.

Keep your questions simple. Stick to one type of question. When you lump the two types of questions together, you run the risk that your customers may not register all the responses they need to give. If a question is long and involved, break it down. When you need to ask a series of questions, try interjecting some of the following statements in place of questions, so you will not sound as though you are interrogating your customer with a barrage of questions.

"Tell me about. . . ."

"Tell me more."

"I'd like to get more information on. . . ."

"Describe. . . ."

Ask open questions when you need information. Questions that require more than a one-word or short answer will get the customer talking. Use open questions when you begin the questioning process to encourage your customer to talk. Open questions begin with what, why, and how.

"How do you. . . ."

"What would you like. . . ."

"What else. . . ."

"What are. . . ."

"Why is that. . . ."

"How are you. . . ."

"What would happen. . . ."

"How will. . . ."

"What type. . . ."

TIP

Be careful when asking a "why" question. For example, the question "Why do you want to do that?" may put your customer on the defensive. She might reply, "It's none of your business." Smiling and using a reflective or helpful tone indicates you are asking out of interest to learn more about your customer's needs.

Ask Closed Questions to Control the Conversation

When you need short answers to clarify information or when you need a specific yes or no, choose closed questions. Questions beginning with "is," "are," "do," "can," or "will" require only a yes or no answer. Questions beginning with "who," "would," "how," or "where" require a short answer. Closed questions are good to use toward the end of the questioning portion of your contact to narrow down the information you need to help your customer.

"*Are you. . . .*"

"*Do you think. . . .*"

"*Will you. . . .*"

"*Would you like. . . .*"

"*Where do you. . . .*"

"*How many. . . .*"

"*Who will. . . .*"

Before Answering a Customer's Question, Make Sure You Understand It

If you do not clearly understand a customer's question, recap it or ask a clarifying question rather than guessing at an answer. It is better to ask another question than to answer the wrong question. Also, never answer a question unless you are sure your answer is accurate. It is better to say "I don't know" than to give an answer that may be incorrect. If you do not know, say so; follow up with "I'll find out for you." Remember to always focus on what you *can* do, rather than on what you *can't*. If a customer asks you to do something you cannot do, say, "Here's what I can do for you...."

TIP

> When a customer asks for another employee who is not available, never say that the employee is at lunch, on break, went home early, has not come in yet, or that you do not know where the employee is. Rather, say, "_____ is unavailable now. How can I help you?" or "_____ is out of the office now. I'll be happy to help you."

Try to Give More Than a One-Word Answer

No matter which questioning technique customers use, answer as though the question is open ended. Try to give customers sufficient information to help them make decisions. Giving more than a one-word answer can have an added bonus: You can generate sales. For example, if Steve asks, "Do you have potato salad?," the employee can answer "Yes." Or . . . "We sure do. We also have coleslaw, baked beans, and pasta salad." Now Steve has many options from which to choose. He may decide to order not only the potato salad, but other sides as well, helping to improve the deli's bottom line.

BRAINSTORM

> As a group, discuss the reasons you might need to ask questions of your customers. Together, come up with typical open and closed questions you should ask to best serve their needs.
>
> Answering questions with more than one-word answers can be difficult at times. Think about some closed questions your customers might ask you and come up with answers that are more than yes or no.

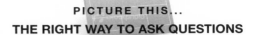

PICTURE THIS...
THE RIGHT WAY TO ASK QUESTIONS

Steve finished his order. ". . . a ham on rye with mustard and a pastrami on rye with mustard."

"What else would you like?"

"Do you have potato salad?"

"We sure do. We also have cole slaw, baked beans, and pasta salad."

"I'll take a side order of potato salad."

"Would you like any other sides?"

"No thanks."

"No problem. Just one more thing. Do you want spicy or regular mustard on the sandwiches?"

"Regular."

How Did the Customer Feel?

Because the employee asked a combination of open and closed questions, Steve felt confident that the order had been written down correctly. He also appreciated the employee asking him if he wanted anything else.

STEP 5
WHEN THE CUSTOMER SAYS NO

You will absolutely, definitely, positively, have to handle customers who say no. When you offer a valid solution and your customer says no, your job is to uncover the reasons for your customer's objections. If you work in sales, it may also be your job to find ways to convince the customer to say yes. The bottom line, always, is to do what is right for your customer. Never offer or try to sell a customer something he or she does not need just to make a sale. When you get to the real reason for the objection, you will figure out the best solution for that particular customer.

Listen to the Customer's Objection

When a customer says no, an objection is made to your proposed solution. To learn the reason behind the no, ask a combination of open and closed questions. You need to understand why the customer is saying no so you can best help him or her. For example, you just made a sales proposal for a complete home security system, and the customer says no. You might ask, "What type of security are you interested in for your home?" The customer's responses might be: "Something a little cheaper" or "This one seems too complicated for my needs."

Acknowledge the Objection

Always validate the customer's reason, and then respond with a positive statement. For example: "I can understand the price may seem high, but our system offers full security in case of fire and break-in. When you consider that, it isn't as expensive as it seems." Or, "At first it may seem complicated, but once you learn how to use it, it becomes second nature." Doing this shows that you empathize with the customer's objection, while adding another benefit to the solution you proposed.

Follow Up with a Question

The customer objected. You listened to the customer's objection, acknowledged it, and gave more information about your proposal. Next, you need to follow up. "How does that sound?" "What do you think about that?" By following up with a clarifying question, you will know how to proceed.

Consider the Customer's Answer

The customer's response will determine whether she is objecting because she does not agree with your proposal or whether she is looking for more information. If the customer responds with something like, "How much did you say it will cost?," she is interested in more information about the product. However, if she answers, "I really can't afford that," proceed with caution. If you have other products to offer, you can ask, "What were you looking to spend?" The customer's response will help you determine whether to continue.

TIP

Always be truthful when stating your point of view or the benefits of a product. In other words, never try to make a sale or glorify the point you are attempting to make just to get the customer to agree with you. When you are not truthful, you will come across in a phony manner and the customer will figure out what you are doing.

PICTURE THIS...
THE RIGHT WAY TO HANDLE OBJECTIONS

"Would you like any other sides?" the deli employee asked.

"No thanks," Steve responded.

"Nothing for anyone else?"

"No one mentioned anything. I wouldn't know what to order."

"I understand, but potato salad would be a good choice. We do have a larger size."

"Hmm, I'm not sure."

"The larger size only costs a dollar more than the price for the side order size. How does that sound?"

"Only a dollar more? OK, that sounds good."

"Great. Just one more thing, do you want spicy or regular mustard?"

"Regular."

How Did the Customer Feel?

Steve liked the fact that even though he said no, the employee gave him another option, then asked a follow-up question. If the employee hadn't asked, Steve wouldn't have thought about ordering the larger size, and he was glad he did.

STEP 6
LISTENING ACTIVELY

In Step 1, you learned that it is impossible to speak and listen at the same time and do both well. Speaking is important because you are delivering a message, but listening is often more important because, without the ability to listen carefully, communication can never be effective. If you do not listen to the message, you might easily give the wrong response.

Focus Entirely on Your Customer

Think of the customer you are helping as the only customer in your business. When you do this, you will be able to give him or her your full attention. When you are listening to the customer, stay interested, even if your customer's message is long. When that happens, you can show empathy in your facial expressions or by nodding to indicate that you are following what the customer is saying. When you nod occasionally and say something like, "I see," "tell me more," or "hmm," you show you are still listening. If your customer rambles or gets off track, you may politely interrupt and ask some clarifying questions to take control of the conversation.

Listen Completely

When you try to listen and talk at the same time, you do neither effectively. Pay attention to the speaker. You are going to get the ball tossed back to you and, when it is your turn to speak, you will want the other person to pay attention. Try not to think of your response when the speaker is still talking. Wait until the message is winding down before thinking how you want to respond. Unless you hear the customer's complete statement or question, you might come up with the incorrect response.

Handle Interruptions Professionally

If someone interrupts you, and it is an avoidable interruption, explain to the interrupter that you will be with him as soon as you are done helping your customer. If it is an unavoidable interruption, excuse yourself momentarily from your customer to answer the other person. Then quickly return your attention and apologize for the interruption.

Remain Objective; Do Not Judge

Before drawing a conclusion or making a judgment, gather as much information as you can. This will help you avoid jumping to conclusions. If you are not sure you understand correctly, paraphrase the customer's words or ask more questions to gather additional information

TIP

Never assume you know what your customers want. If you are unsure, ask a clarifying question.

Listen for What Is Not Said

You learned about nonverbal communication and how important it is to pay attention to your mannerisms. It is also important to pay attention to your customers' nonverbal signals to see if their words match their emotions. Pay attention to what your customers are really saying. If a customer appears on edge, upset, or angry, show empathy in your replies.

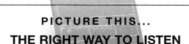

PICTURE THIS...
THE RIGHT WAY TO LISTEN

"OK, you mentioned you were in a hurry so I'll put a rush on your order," the deli employee told Steve. "It should be out very soon."

Throughout their interaction, the employee made eye contact as he wrote down Steve's order. He also asked questions to clarify the order. And, since he could tell Steve was in a hurry, he responded accordingly.

How Did the Customer Feel?

Because Steve felt he received great customer service, he thought, *I'm going to come here more often for lunch.*

PICTURE THIS...
PUTTING IT ALL TOGETHER

Steve stopped at the local deli for lunch. He was in a hurry to place the order for himself and his coworkers and was greeted by an employee who looked at him, smiled, and enthusiastically said, "Hi, welcome to Max's Deli. How are you doing?"

"I'm doing great, thanks, but I am in a hurry. Is it possible to get my order quickly?"

"Yes, absolutely. I'll put a rush on it. What can I get you?"

Steve began to give his order. "I'll have a turkey and Swiss on whole wheat with mayo and tomatoes. . . ." As he spoke, he noticed that the employee looked directly at him before writing down the item. He smiled often, his posture told Steve he was interested, and he nodded occasionally as Steve spoke.

Steve finished his order. ". . . a ham on rye with mustard and a pastrami on rye with mustard."

"What else would you like?"

"Do you have potato salad?"

"We sure do. We also have cole slaw, baked beans, and pasta salad."

"I'll take a side order of potato salad."

"Would you like any other sides?" the deli employee asked.

"No thanks," Steve responded.

"Nothing for anyone else?"

"No one mentioned anything. I wouldn't know what to order."

"I understand, but potato salad would be a good choice. We do have a larger size."

"Hmm, I'm not sure."

"The larger size only costs a dollar more than the price for the side order size. How does that sound?"

"Only a dollar more? OK, that sounds good."

"Great. Just one more thing. Do you want spicy or regular mustard?"

"Regular."

"OK, you mentioned you were in a hurry so I'll put a rush on your order," the deli employee told Steve. "It should be out very soon."

No matter where you work, you can apply the principles of communicating effectively to your interactions with your customers. Think before you speak, be aware of your nonverbal messages, use good grammar, ask the correct questions and answer questions correctly, handle objections effectively, and above all, listen, listen, listen.

In Your Dealings with Customers, Be the One to Initiate Honest, Respectful, and Thoughtful Communication

It's happened to all of us. Someone you thought you knew—perhaps a friend or a family member—did something dishonest or disrespectful to you, causing you to lose trust in that person. When trust is lost, it takes a long time to regain it. The same goes for business dealings. Unlike personal relationships, where working to rebuild trust is vital to maintain the relationship, customers won't give you a second chance if they feel they have been lied to or disrespected. Can you afford to lose your customers? Think about it. In today's uncertain business climate, holding on to your existing customers is more important than ever. When you communicate truthfully and respectfully, you send a powerful message—you show your customers that you value and appreciate them, and they are far more likely to value and appreciate you.

- Actions always speak louder than words.

- Honesty is always the best policy.

- To your customers, *you* are the company.

- Represent your company well by communicating effectively.

- Never do anything to cause a customer to lose trust in you.

K E Y   P O I N T S

Step 1: Saying What You Mean and Meaning What You Say

- Choose the right words.
- Make sure your tone fits the message you are sending.
- Add welcome words to your vocabulary.
- Keep business conversations professional.

Step 2: What You Don't Say: Nonverbal Communication

- Actions speak louder than words.
- Smile often.
- Make eye contact.
- Maintain a relaxed, open demeanor.
- Keep your energy level steady.

Step 3: Putting Words Together: Grammar Usage

- Reflect your company's personality.
- Speak clearly.
- Use everyday language.
- Avoid using slang, jargon, company terms, and technical language.

Step 4: Asking the Correct Questions and Answering the Questions Correctly

- Keep your questions simple.
- Ask open questions when you need information.
- Ask closed questions to control the conversation.
- Before answering a customer's question, make sure you understand it.
- Try to give more than a one-word answer.

Step 5: When the Customer Says No

- Listen to the customer's objection.
- Acknowledge the objection.
- Follow up with a question.
- Consider the customer's answer.

Step 6: Listening Actively

- Focus entirely on your customer.
- Listen completely.
- Handle interruptions professionally.
- Remain objective; do not judge.
- Listen for what is not said.

PRACTICE LESSON

Step 1: Saying What You Mean and Meaning What You Say

Make a list of words and phrases you will incorporate into your vocabulary.

_____

_____

_____

Step 2: What You Don't Say: Nonverbal Communication

Give examples of what you will do to improve your nonverbal communication skills.

_____

_____

_____

Step 3: Putting Words Together: Grammar Usage

Think about your grammar and list some things you can do to improve it.

_____

_____

_____

Step 4: Asking the Correct Questions and Answering the Questions Correctly

Think about your typical customer contacts and write examples of open and closed questions you will use.

_____

_____

_____

Step 5: When the Customer Says No

Think about a recent customer contact in which the customer had an objection. Using the questioning techniques, explain how you would handle the customer.

_____

_____

_____

Step 6: Listening Actively

Give examples of how you plan to improve your listening skills.

_____

_____

_____

D O I N G   I T   R I G H T !

I've been doing business with Donna for almost two years now. She is my go-to person for print jobs. The first time we met, I had an unusual job to complete. I drove to Staples and as I explained what I wanted, Donna looked directly at me, listened well, and paid attention as I showed her the document. She asked some questions to clear up any possible confusion and took notes as I answered. She assured me that she would take care of my job. I knew I was in good hands.

Later that day Donna called me. "I started printing out your job but the pages look odd to me. Before I continue, I just want to double-check that I have this right…." I answered her questions, assured her she did have it right, and thanked her for calling to check.

When I drove to pick up my order, I was confident that it would be done correctly. I wasn't disappointed. "I really appreciate that you took the time to call yesterday," I complimented Donna. "That meant a lot to me."

"It just looked so weird," she said with a smile. "I didn't want you to drive all the way here only to find out I had done it wrong." That was the exact moment that I knew I could rely on Donna. For someone to care that much told me that she truly valued me as a customer.

Other companies might be less expensive. They might even have a quicker turn-around time. That doesn't really matter to me. When you find someone good you stay with her. You see, Donna might be a Staples employee, but to me Donna *is* Staples—and she represents her company well.

H O W   D O   I   M E A S U R E   U P ?

1. When I communicate with my customers, do I remember to think
    before I speak to ensure that I choose the right words? What inter-
    nal cues can I use to always present myself professionally?

    _____

    _____

    _____

2. What nonverbal messages am I sending? What am I good at? What
    can I do to improve?

    _____

    _____

    _____

3. How is my grammar? What are my bad habit "words," and what can
    I do to stop using them?

    _____

    _____

    _____

4. Do I ask a combination of open and closed questions to make sure I
    understand my customers' requests? In the typical situations where I
    stumble, what can I do to correct myself?

    _____

    _____

    _____

3

Jumping in with Both Feet: Relationship Building

TO PROVIDE THE BEST POSSIBLE SERVICE, YOU MUST GET CLOSE TO YOUR CUSTOMERS BY BUILDING A STRONG RELATIONSHIP WITH THEM

Did you know that every customer contact results in a relationship? Even when customers only do business with a company once, they remember and judge the company based on their relationship with its employees. They remember whether their relationship is good or bad, and they are also likely to share their experiences with others. As a result, your customers can be your best—or your worst—marketing and advertising tools.

CUSTOMER SERVICE IS BUILDING RELATIONSHIPS

Relationship building is the cornerstone of customer service. Remember, to your customers you are the company. So from the moment customers form their first impression to the moment you complete your interaction with them, you have a valuable opportunity to build a strong relationship. The same applies to those customers who may only visit once or sporadically. When you interact positively and go out of your way to help each customer, you build a relationship. And when those customers receive great service, they will remember and tell others about their positive experiences.

When you are courteous and have a positive attitude toward your customers, you show that you care. When you demonstrate good communication skills by thinking before you speak, keeping your nonverbal body language relaxed and open, and using correct grammar, you present yourself as intelligent and confident. When you ask the correct questions to help the customer and answer any and all questions the customer asks, you present yourself as a competent employee. When listening carefully, you demonstrate that you are truly interested in each and every customer.

So far you are off to a good start in learning how to provide great customer service. The next step is learning how to build relationships.

You interact with customers in two ways. You work to build new relationships as well as to maintain ongoing relationships. Without new business relationships, your company will not grow. Without ongoing business relationships, you will not develop the loyal customer base that will allow you to maintain your existing business.

Building and maintaining positive relationships is based on the principles of basic courtesies and effective communication. Your relationship begins when a customer forms a first impression of you and your company. It continues when you establish a rapport. Think for a moment about a personal relationship you are or were in. When you first met that special person, you probably made small talk to see if you had something in common. When you discovered that you shared common interests and common ground, you made the decision to take your relationship to the next level by going on a date.

Although the purpose of business relationships is not to result in dates, during those first few minutes with a customer it is equally important to find common ground to begin building your relationship. Establishing a rapport with your customer is the first step. You can do this by asking a question as simple as, "How are you today?," and then listening to the customer's response.

From these first few words with a customer, you have the opportunity to respond in a positive and upbeat manner. If the customer says he or she is not doing well at all, you may respond, "I'm sorry to hear that. How can I help you?" Showing interest helps to establish a rapport.

When you are helpful and interested in finding the right solution for your customers, you interact positively. Identifying what the customer needs and then doing all you can to take care of their request will make each customer feel valued.

When customers offer you repeat business, you have the opportunity to maintain an ongoing relationship by remembering them, by remembering something about them, and by learning their tastes and preferences. And for the customer who was not having a good day before, you might say, "Hi Mrs. Adams, I hope you're having a better day today." Think how special Mrs. Adams will feel knowing that she was important enough to you to remember something about her.

In business, you will deal with many different types of customers. Learning how to interact positively with various personality types will enable you to handle any type of customer in any type of situation. You will be on your way to knowing how to establish and maintain long-term, high-quality relationships with all your customers.

Before we jump in with both feet and learn how to build and maintain positive relationships, we need to take a step back and identify the answers to three important questions that will help you to understand your customers:

- Who are your customers?

- What do they expect from your business?

- How do your products and services enhance their lives?

Discuss and answer these questions. Then you will have a better idea of how to establish a rapport with your customers because you already have general information about them. This will give you the information needed to find common ground and begin building relationships.

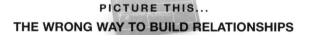

PICTURE THIS...
THE WRONG WAY TO BUILD RELATIONSHIPS

Sarah was an unlikely customer service employee. She was home from college for summer break and took a part-time job at a women's clothing shop in the local mall. Sarah had not worked in retail before, and she was unsure about how to interact with customers. Her job was to greet customers and help them find what they needed. On her first day, her manager explained her job duties, showed her where to locate stock in the backroom, and told her to be friendly to customers.

"Be sure you say hello to the customers when they come in," her manager said as she walked away.

Sarah busied herself folding tops on the front display table.

Beth Adams, meanwhile, was outside the store looking at the clothing display in the window. She came into the store and noticed Sarah.

This was Sarah's first customer. She nervously said "Hi," barely speaking above a whisper as she quickly glanced at the woman and then back down to her work. Sarah continued to fold the tops while the woman browsed.

"Excuse me, can you see if you have this skirt in a size twelve?" Beth asked.

Sarah nodded, took the item from Beth, and retreated into the stock room without saying a word or making eye contact. When Sarah came back she said, "Sorry, we don't have it." She spoke softly and looked at the floor as she spoke.

"Oh, all right. Well, thanks for checking." Beth walked out of the store.

What Went Wrong?

Even though Sarah knew she would have to deal with customers, she did not understand the importance of building relationships. She wanted to work in this clothing store to get the employee discount and had not thought about her duties or the customers.

Sarah's manager assumed she knew how to interact well with customers, but if they had discussed the answers to the three questions above, Sarah would have known who her customers were and whether they were sporadic shoppers or regular customers.

The manager and Sarah should have discussed customers' expectations. Then Sarah would have known how involved she was supposed to become with the store's customers. She would have also understood whether her job duties involved helping customers select outfits or whether they should be allowed to browse without assistance. In addition, she needed to understand if she should expect to be interacting with the same customers regularly and if she needed to introduce herself and get to know their individual tastes and styles.

Moreover, the manager should have explained to Sarah how the store's products enhance its customers' lives. Knowing this would enable Sarah to help her customers more effectively. If this was an expensive boutique where the customers were interested in designer labels, Sarah could show customers where to find specific items. If the store stocked trendy clothes, Sarah could show customers the newest items and the hot sellers.

The responsibility for what went wrong in this scenario lies both with Sarah and her manager. Although her manager showed Sarah where to locate stock in the backroom, how to keep the displays neat, and told her to be friendly to the customers, did she make sure Sarah understood? Likewise, did Sarah ask questions to make sure she understood her job responsibilities? Unless she knew specifically how she was supposed to interact with customers, Sarah most likely felt she was doing her job correctly.

How Did the Customer Feel?

Sarah did not make a good first impression. She should have made eye contact, smiled, and greeted Beth in a friendly, helpful manner. When Beth asked for a specific skirt, she got the impression that Sarah was not interested in helping her. To change that, Sarah could have said, "I'll be happy to check on that," or "Absolutely. I'll be glad to see if we have that." Because Sarah acted disinterested, Beth did not feel valued and she was ambivalent about going back to that store.

By learning the six steps below you will learn how to build and maintain positive and strong relationships with all your customers.

Step 1: Establishing Rapport

Step 2: Interacting Positively with Customers

Step 3: Identifying Customers' Needs

Step 4: Making the Customer Feel Valued

Step 5: Maintaining Ongoing Relationships

Step 6: Different Strokes: Handling Different Types of Customers

Doing a good job and building strong relationships is a two-way street. Both the manager and the employee need to be clear on customer expectations. Asking and answering questions will uncover any inconsistencies.

Even in a store where customers may only visit occasionally, employees can develop relationships with them. Every customer interaction, even short-term ones, results in a relationship.

STEP 1
ESTABLISHING RAPPORT

Establishing a rapport begins the moment you start communicating with your customers. Smiling at a customer can help establish a rapport by showing you are interested. How you establish a rapport depends on your customer interactions. Think about your place of employment and the answers you identified in the Brainstorm on page 71:

> *Who are my customers?* Are they men, women, tweens, teens, young adults, or all age groups?

> *What do they expect from my company?* Do they expect quality products? Good value? The best prices? Quick service? Products that will enhance their self-images? A large selection? The latest styles?

> *How do my company's products and services enhance the customers' lives?* Do they make the customers' lives easier? Are they a necessity? Do they make our customers feel good about themselves?

When you can answer these questions, you will have a good idea about how to relate to your customers. Armed with this knowledge, you can begin to establish a rapport with them, which is the first step in relationship building. Every relationship begins by laying building blocks on top of the basic foundation you learned in Chapter 1.

Be Friendly

No matter who your customers are, everyone appreciates someone who is friendly. When you smile and offer a friendly greeting, you put your customers at ease. You show them, from the start, that you are a person who is approachable and willing to help.

Be Interested

The smile and greeting also show that you are interested. When you ask people how they are doing or how you can help, you are enhancing the message that you are interested. Being interested means listening when customers respond to your approach. Imagine how you would sound if you asked a customer how he was doing and he said, "I'm having the worst day of my life. Really awful," and with no emotion you responded, "Oh," or worse, made no comment at all. The customer most likely would be wondering why you bothered to ask. Being interested means listening and responding accordingly. Being interested means thinking of ways to brighten other people's days.

Be Considerate

If a customer says he is having the worst day of his life, you might say, "I'm sorry to hear that. What can I do to make your day better?" Not only are you showing interest, but you are showing you are sensitive to the customer's situation. Even if you cannot personally understand or relate to what the customer is saying, you can be considerate in your response.

Be Trustful

The best way to demonstrate that you can be trusted is by being honest and ethical in everything you do. When you act with integrity, your personality reflects your honesty. If you are friendly and helpful with a customer and later make fun of him within earshot of other customers, you do not come across as being a trustful person. Being trustful includes treating people with dignity and respect.

Find Common Ground

When you listen to your customer's statements and responses, try to find something you have in common. To the customer who is having a bad day, you might respond, "I'm sorry to hear that. I had one of those days yesterday. Nothing seemed to go right for me." The customer will appreciate that you can relate to his experience. Even if you did not have a bad day to relate to, there are other ways to find common ground. Empathize with the customer. Ask a question. Show interest. In other situations, you can relate by complimenting the customer on something she is wearing, by saying something about yourself, or even by talking about the weather.

PICTURE THIS...
THE RIGHT WAY TO ESTABLISH RAPPORT

"Be sure you say hello to the customers when they come in," her manager said as she walked away.

Sarah stopped her and asked, "When I say hi to customers, am I supposed to ask if they need help or should I leave them alone?"

"That's a good question. Most of our customers are working women who come in to browse so we usually leave them alone. But I do want you to let them know you are here to help if they need anything. When a customer comes in, smile, look at her, and say something like, 'Hi, how are you today? If you need anything, I'll be happy to help you find it.' That way the customer knows we're going to leave her alone to browse, but will be available to help."

"OK." Sarah busied herself folding tops on the front display table.

Beth Adams, meanwhile, was outside the store looking at the clothing display in the window. She came into the store and noticed Sarah.

This was Sarah's first customer. She was nervous, but knew what she needed to do. She looked at Beth, smiled, and said, "Hi, how are you doing today?"

Beth smiled back. "I'm fine, thanks, how are you?"

"It's my first day, so I don't know yet. I'm a little nervous."

"I know how that feels. I'm sure you'll do just fine."

"If you need anything, I'll be happy to help you find it."

"Thanks, I'm looking for a skirt. I'll look around."

"OK. We have skirts in great summer colors."

Beth smiled and walked away.

How Did the Customer Feel?

Even though Sarah felt awkward, she showed she was friendly by smiling and greeting Beth. Beth appreciated the interest Sarah displayed by listening and commenting on the skirts in great summer colors. When she told Beth it was her first day and she was nervous, Beth could relate to her feelings and they found common ground. Beth felt comfortable with Sarah, who established a rapport with her.

STEP 2
INTERACTING POSITIVELY WITH CUSTOMERS

Once you establish a rapport, continue building your relationships by interacting with your customers in a positive manner. When you are positive and upbeat, people will respond similarly. It is hard to stay down with someone who is upbeat. Think about the type of people you like to be around. We tend to gravitate to people who bring us up, not those who want to drag us down. At work, be a person who brings others up.

Be Helpful

Show your customers you care. Go the extra mile for them. Do something to make other people feel good about themselves. Set a personal goal to help someone every day. You will feel better when you meet that goal. It is a great personal habit to get into.

Be Committed

When you commit yourself to your company and your customers, you will look for ways to make things better. No matter what you do today, do your best. Give today and every day your all. Give your customers your all.

Be a Problem Solver

Be part of the solution rather than part of the problem. Look for answers rather than focusing on what is wrong. When you adopt a problem-solving approach, you will find it hard to be negative. People who focus on problems complain; people who focus on solutions find ways to make things better.

Be Credible

This means being knowledgeable about your products and your company. Customers appreciate nice employees, but they also value knowledgeable employees. Learn as much as you can about your product line. If you need additional technical training, ask your manager for it.

Believe in Your Products

No matter what your company manufactures or sells, whether it is life insurance or clothing, you need to believe in your products. Otherwise, you will never come across sincerely. Sincerity is based on believing in what you do. Believing that your products will help your customers is crucial to doing the right thing for them. It does not matter what line of work you are in, when you truly believe that your company's products can help your customers, you will promote your products, your company, and yourself in a positive and sincere manner.

PICTURE THIS...
THE RIGHT WAY TO INTERACT POSITIVELY

Sarah continued to fold the tops while Beth browsed.

"Excuse me, can you see if you have this skirt in a size twelve?" Beth asked.

Sarah took the skirt from Beth and said, "Yes, I'll be happy to. This is a great skirt, and I love this shade of green."

"I love it too. I hope you have it, I could use a green skirt."

"I'll be right back." Sarah hurried into the stock room. She came back with a different style green skirt and said, "I'm sorry, we don't have that skirt in your size. I don't know if you saw this one. I brought it because you mentioned you wanted a green skirt."

"Thanks, but that isn't exactly what I was looking for."

How Did the Customer Feel?

Beth felt that Sarah was helpful and, because Sarah demonstrated she was solution oriented by bringing a different green skirt for consideration, Beth had a positive feeling about her.

STEP 3
IDENTIFYING CUSTOMERS' NEEDS

Customers come into your business for a reason. Sometimes they are not very clear about their needs. Beth was specific when she mentioned she needed a green skirt. This helped Sarah come up with an alternative option. If Beth had not mentioned a green skirt, Sarah would not have known her needs. While this is a simplistic example, the principle is the same, whether you sell clothing or computer systems. When you deal with customers, your job is to uncover their needs.

Ask Questions

In Chapter 2, you learned about open and closed questions. When customers do not know how to tell you what they need, it is your job to figure it out. Sometimes customers are not even sure they know what they need. Use open questions to get the customer talking. Remember, questions that begin with "what," "why," and "how" encourage customers to talk. Use closed questions to clarify an answer. Closed questions begin with "who," "would," "how," and "where." A question beginning with "how" can be either open or closed: Open: "How do you think you would use this?" Closed: "How many times a week will you use it?"

Summarize Customers' Needs

After you have asked enough questions to determine your customer's needs, summarize your understanding of what he or she has told you. For example, "From what I understand, your son has allergies, and you are looking for a vacuum cleaner that will remove the greatest number of allergens and is the least costly" or "You mentioned that you got your bill, and you were overcharged for. . . ." If your understanding is incorrect, ask more open and closed questions until you get it right.

Recommend Appropriate Solutions

When you ask enough questions, you get enough information to recommend the best solution. If your job is to sell products, you can make an appropriate proposal. If you handle billing issues and miscellaneous problems, you can find a workable solution. Make sure that your recommendations are based on what the customer told you. Refer to things the customer said when making your recommendation. "This is our most economical vacuum, and it will remove 99 percent of all allergens. With your son's allergies, you want to make sure your vacuum picks up as many allergen particles as possible."

Handle Objections

Follow the steps you learned in Chapter 2. Listen to the customer's objection. Acknowledge it. Follow up with a question. Consider the customer's answer. If, following up on the vacuum cleaner sale, the customer says "Thanks, I'll think about it," you can respond, "What questions do you have about this one?" "None, but it's more than I wanted to spend." "I can understand that, but this product is the most efficient for removing allergens. We do have cheaper models that I can show you, but none of them work as well as this one."

TIP

Always answer your customer's question, "What is this going to do for me?" Whenever you propose a solution, your customer is silently answering this question. If you know where your customer is coming from it will be easier for you to help him or her find the right solution.

PICTURE THIS...
THE RIGHT WAY TO IDENTIFY CUSTOMERS' NEEDS

"Thanks, but that isn't exactly what I was looking for."

"What type of skirt are you interested in?"

"I prefer longer skirts."

"What other colors would you be interested in?"

"I really wanted green, but I suppose I could use a khaki one, too."

"Do you like prints?"

"No, I only wear solids."

"OK, a longer skirt in a solid green or khaki. Why don't I check in the back to see if we have any?"

"Would you? That would be great."

How Did the Customer Feel?

Beth was pleasantly surprised when Sarah asked her questions to determine exactly what she was looking for, recapped what Beth said to make sure she understood, and made a recommendation to look for another style of skirt. Getting this level of caring service stood out in Beth's mind.

STEP 4
MAKING THE CUSTOMER FEEL VALUED

When you establish a rapport, interact positively, identify customer needs to make a valid recommendation, and make customers feel valued, you are on your way to building strong relationships. Whether your interaction is a one-time conversation or an ongoing interaction with a customer who does repeat business with your company, your primary job is to communicate effectively and build positive relationships.

Go Out of Your Way for Your Customers

Do what you can to help them. Try to give them more than they asked for. When a customer asks a question, give a thorough explanation rather than a one-word answer. Your customers will know when you go out of your way for them. Sarah could have easily let Beth walk out the door when she could not find the skirt she wanted. By going out of her way, she not only made Beth feel valued, she also had the possibility of making a sale.

Validate Customers' Decisions

Even if you do not agree with customers' choices, always validate their decisions. If the vacuum salesperson was not able to make the sale, he could validate the customer's decision by saying, "I understand how you feel. This brand is costly." How would Beth feel if Sarah replied, "You want green? Green is such a drab color. Why not go for a bright color like pink?" Sarah validated Beth's decision to buy a green skirt by saying that was a great color. When she could not find that particular skirt in green she asked Beth what she was interested in. This also validated Beth's feelings.

Instill Positive Feelings

Never make customers feel bad about their decisions. Think how the mother would feel if the salesperson said, "I guess your son will have to deal with the allergens in your house." Rather, he could say, "It's a big decision. I'll be happy to help you if you have any more questions about it."

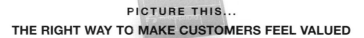

PICTURE THIS...
THE RIGHT WAY TO MAKE CUSTOMERS FEEL VALUED

Sarah returned with a skirt. "I found this khaki skirt. How do you like it?"

After looking it over, Beth said, "Thanks for looking, but I still like the style of the green one better."

"I understand and I appreciate that you really liked that skirt. I'm sorry I couldn't help you find something."

How Did the Customer Feel?

Sarah went out of her way to find another skirt, but when Beth said it was not what she was looking for, Sarah validated Beth's decision by saying she understood. She instilled positive feelings in Beth by assuring her that she appreciated her decision.

STEP 5
MAINTAINING ONGOING RELATIONSHIPS

Once you build strong relationships with customers, your work is not done. In any relationship, whether business or personal, you have to work to maintain it. Customers come back a second time because you established a relationship with them. Imagine how valued they will feel if you remember them? Because Sarah went out of her way to help Beth, Beth is likely to return. That is the way to build customer loyalty. If, on the other hand, Beth goes back and Sarah does not remember her, Beth will not be as likely to come back.

Remember Your Customers

Nothing makes a customer feel more valued than being remembered. Acknowledge your repeat customers by saying something to show you remember them. Customers who do repeat business with a company appreciate being recognized. When customers are treated as though they are invisible, they might just become invisible.

Learn Customers' Names

When customers come into your business repeatedly, make it a point to learn their names. Addressing a customer by name will let her know she is important to you. If you do not know the customer well, use the last name. "Hi Mrs. Adams. How are you today?" Leave it up to Mrs. Adams to tell you whether you should call her by her first name.

TIP

To help remember names, when you are introduced repeat the person's name. "I'm pleased to meet you, Barbara." Use the name a couple times during conversation, "Barbara, you mentioned that...." After the person leaves, think of something that will help you remember the name. For example, you could create an associative memory jogger such as, "Barbara, blue eyes."

Remember Something About Your Customers

Remember the customer who was having the worst day? Think how he would feel if next time you said, "Hi, how are you doing today? I hope you're having a better day than the last time you were in." Everyone appreciates an employee with a good memory. This shows your customers that you value your relationship with them.

Learn Your Customers' Preferences

If you deal with the same customers repeatedly, get to know what they like. If you have too many customers to remember each one's tastes, you could start a card file or a computer file and note your repeat customers' preferences and other information you might want to remember about them. Next time they come in, try to incorporate their preferences into your conversation. Your customers will be impressed that you remembered.

TIP

Try to do something special every now and then for your repeat customers. It can be something as simple as taking the time to talk to them, showing new products that might interest them, or offering a special sale price on a product or service.

PICTURE THIS...
THE RIGHT WAY TO MAINTAIN ONGOING RELATIONSHIPS

The following week, Sarah spotted Beth in the store. She walked over to her. "Hi. You know I thought of you the other day."

"You did?"

"I sure did. We got some new green skirts in, and I was hoping I'd see you. We still have some in stock. Would you like me to show them to you?"

"Yes! I can't believe you remembered."

How Did the Customer Feel?

Beth was wowed that Sarah not only remembered her, but that she remembered she was looking for a green skirt. Sarah built a relationship with Beth and now she is working to maintain it. Because she was wowed, next time Beth needs clothes, where do you think she will go?

S T E P   6

DIFFERENT STROKES: HANDLING DIFFERENT TYPES OF CUSTOMERS

Most of your customers will be average people with average needs. Most of your customers will be pleasant people who appreciate your help. Some customers, though, will test your skills and, at times, your patience, and customers with disabilities may make you feel uncomfortable because you are afraid you will do or say something wrong.

Besides the average, everyday people with whom you regularly interact, here are some other customer types, as well as some tips on how to interact positively with them.

The Pushy, Obnoxious Customer—Remain Calm

Maintain a professional demeanor. Smile. Try to put the customer at ease. Speak softly, and control your voice inflection. Never take on the same tone this type of customer uses with you. Speak in a positive, upbeat tone of voice. When you stay calm, you stay in control. When you stay in control, you will be able to help this type of customer without coming unglued. Remember that pushy, obnoxious customers do not act this way only with you. This behavior is part of their personalities. Perhaps being pushy is the only way they know how to act. In other words, do not take their behavior personally.

The Timid, Indecisive Customer—Be Patient

Help draw these customers out and get them to talk more. Ask open-ended questions. Listen closely to their responses, and guide them to give you the information needed to help them reach a decision. Some people have a difficult time making any decision. Some people are naturally shy. Be sensitive to timid, indecisive customers, and help them become more talkative by asking questions and encouraging them to talk.

The Overly Friendly, Flirty Customer—Be Professional

Keep your end of the conversation on business. These customers can be difficult to handle because they do not see their behavior as inappropriate. It is up to you to control the conversation. Do not foster overly friendly or flirty behavior by being overly friendly in return. Guide your conversation back to business. If a flirty customer continues, offer a gentle reminder that you want to help—with a business solution.

The Culturally Different Customer—Be Tolerant

We live in a society that incorporates many cultures, languages, and customs, yet people often do not know how to talk or act in the presence of a person with a different background. Displaying kindness, smiling, and being honest and courteous translate into any language and across any barrier. People who do not look like us or act like we do can make us uncomfortable. By learning to be tolerant of differences, you will overcome any cultural obstacles.

People with Disabilities—Be Respectful

Treat them like you treat anyone else. Make eye contact and speak in your normal tone and pace of speech. Focus on the person first and the disability second. Putting the disability first, such as saying "the handicapped person," places the focus on the disability rather than on the person. When referring to a person with a disability, use terms such as "the man who uses a wheelchair," "the woman who is blind," or "the person with epilepsy." Once you get used to dealing with people with disabilities, you will see that they want to be treated like anyone else, with dignity and respect.

TIP

> Terms such as "crippled," "retarded," "deformed," "lame," or "crazy" are never acceptable, so drop these and other words with negative connotations from your vocabulary. If you do not know how to refer to a person, use the term "person with a disability."

Here are some other suggestions as to how you should interact with people with disabilities:

- Offer to shake hands if this is normally how you greet people. It is acceptable to shake a person's left hand. If, after offering your hand, you find the person is unable to shake hands, complete the hand-shake by placing your hand on the person's right hand.

- Always ask first if a person wants help: "I'll be happy to reach that if you'd like."

- If you don't know what to do to help a person, ask what you should do: "I'd like to help you. Please tell me what I can do."

For people who use wheelchairs:

- Try to place yourself at the person's eye level if you are going to have a lengthy conversation.

- Never lean on a wheelchair or hover over the person.

- Make eye contact and speak directly to the person, not to the person's companion.

For people with developmental or cognitive disabilities:

- Speak clearly and use short, easy-to-understand words.

- If the person has difficulty writing, offer to help complete any paperwork: "If you'd like, I'll be happy to fill out the application for you."

- Give the person ample time to formulate thoughts and respond to you.

- Refrain from finishing the person's sentence.

For people with visual impairments:

- Never touch a service dog without first asking permission.

- Tell the person about any obstacles in his or her path: "There are boxes in the aisle ahead, so we'll walk on the left side."

- When asking the person to take a seat, help him or her touch the chair first.

- Verbalize what you are doing to help the person: "I'm inputting the information into my computer so I can give you an installation date."

For people with hearing impairments:

- Look at the person and speak and enunciate clearly.

- Use simple words and short sentences.

For people with speech impairments:

- Ask the person to repeat if you do not understand, then repeat his/her words back to be sure you understood correctly.

- Use closed questions that require short answers.

TIP

In all cases, when interacting with people with disabilities, be patient. Also, don't be embarrassed or overly apologetic if you make a blunder.

When you learn to interact with different types of people and personalities, you will confidently handle any customer in any situation. By building and maintaining positive relationships, you are on your way to providing great customer service.

PICTURE THIS...
PUTTING IT ALL TOGETHER

After being trained, Sarah busied herself folding tops on the front display table.

Beth Adams, meanwhile, was outside the store looking at the clothing display in the window. She came into the store and noticed Sarah.

This was Sarah's first customer. She was nervous, but knew what she needed to do. She looked at Beth, smiled, and said, "Hi, how are you doing today?"

Beth smiled back. "I'm fine, thanks, how are you?"

"It's my first day so I don't know yet. I'm a little nervous."

"I know how that feels. I'm sure you'll do just fine."

"If you need anything, I'll be happy to help you find it."

"Thanks, I'm looking for a skirt. I'll look around."

"OK. We have skirts in great summer colors."

Beth smiled and walked away. Sarah continued to fold the tops while Beth browsed.

"Excuse me, can you see if you have this skirt in a size twelve?" Beth asked.

Sarah took the skirt from Beth and said, "Yes, I'll be happy to. This is a great skirt, and I love this shade of green."

"I love it too. I hope you have it, I could use a green skirt."

"I'll be right back." Sarah hurried into the stock room. She came back with a different style green skirt and said, "I'm sorry, we don't have that skirt in your size. I don't know if you saw this one. I brought it because you mentioned you wanted a green skirt."

"Thanks, but that isn't exactly what I was looking for."

"What type of skirt are you interested in?"

"I prefer longer skirts."

"What other colors would you be interested in?"

"I really wanted green, but I suppose I could use a khaki one, too."

"Do you like prints?"

"No, I only wear solids."

"OK, a longer skirt in a solid green or khaki. Why don't I check in the back to see if we have any?"

"Would you? That would be great." Sarah returned with a skirt. "I found this khaki skirt. How do you like it?"

After looking it over, Beth said, "Thanks for looking, but I still like the style of the green one better."

"I understand and I appreciate that you really liked that skirt. I'm sorry I couldn't help you find something."

The following week, Sarah spotted Beth in the store. She walked over to her. "Hi. You know I thought of you the other day."

"You did?"

"I sure did. We got some new green skirts in, and I was hoping I'd see you. We still have some in stock. Would you like me to show them to you?"

"Yes! I can't believe you remembered."

Your customer interactions may not always be this simple or straightforward. Even if your customer contacts are much more involved, practice these steps and you will be able to build and maintain positive relationships with all your customers.

To Provide the Best Possible Service You Must Get Close to Your Customers by Building a Strong Relationship with Them

As your company's representative—and the face of your business—your number one job is to develop strong customer relationships, whether your customers do business with you repeatedly or are one-time visitors. When you make it your business to give each customer a positive experience, you demonstrate that you care and you show them they are important to you. Every relationship requires ongoing

BUSINESS
NOT
AS USUAL

maintenance, including your customer relationships. When you continually strive to strengthen these relationships, you build strong bonds that result in loyalty. Remember, your customers provide free advertising for you—make sure that what they're saying about you is what you want said about you. When they say good things, you help to "recession proof" your business.

- Tell your customers you appreciate their business.

- Find ways to give them more than they expect.

- Always try to see things from the customer's perspective.

K E Y   P O I N T S

Step 1: Establishing Rapport

- Be friendly.
- Be interested.
- Be sensitive.
- Be trustful.
- Find common ground.

Step 2: Interacting Positively with Customers

- Be helpful.
- Be committed.
- Be a problem solver.
- Be credible.
- Believe in your products.

Step 3: Identifying Customers' Needs

- Ask questions.
- Summarize customers' needs.
- Recommend appropriate solutions.
- Handle objections.

Step 4: Making the Customer Feel Valued

- Go out of your way for your customers.
- Validate customers' decisions.
- Instill positive feelings.

Step 5: Maintaining Ongoing Relationships

- Remember your customers.
- Learn customers' names.

- Remember something about your customers.
- Learn your customers' preferences.

Step 6: Different Strokes: Handling Different Types of Customers

- Pushy, obnoxious customers—remain calm.
- Timid, indecisive customers—be patient.
- Overly friendly, flirty customers—be professional.
- Culturally different customers—be tolerant.
- People with disabilities—be respectful.

PRACTICE LESSON

Step 1: Establishing Rapport

Think of your typical customer. How can you establish a rapport?

_____

_____

Step 2: Interacting Positively with Customers

What are some ways in which you can interact positively with your typical customer?

_____

_____

Step 3: Identifying Customers' Needs

What questions can you ask to uncover your customers' needs?

_____

_____

Step 4: Making the Customer Feel Valued

What are some things you can do to make your customers feel valued?

_____

_____

Step 5: Maintaining Ongoing Relationships

What are some things you can do to make your repeat customers feel special?

_____

_____

Step 6: Different Strokes: Handling Different Types of Customers

How will you handle customers who are:

Pushy and obnoxious

_____

_____

Timid or indecisive

_____

_____

Overly friendly and flirty

_____

_____

Culturally different

_____

_____

Disabled

_____

_____

D O I N G   I T   R I G H T !

If you're old enough, you may remember *Cheers*, the television show about the neighborhood bar where the "regulars" gathered every night. At Cheers, the regulars, the employees, and the owner were like a big extended family. When you think about it, aren't those the types of places you like to go? The places where they always know your name and they're always glad you came?

I'm fortunate to live in an area where we have many restaurants from which to choose. One of my favorites is Sal's Pizzeria. The first time my husband and I walked into his restaurant, Sal paused momentarily from tossing pizza dough to greet us warmly: "Hey folks, thanks for coming in."

His wait staff was equally warm and friendly, smiling and talking with the diners. Clearly, this was a place where Sal and his employees enjoyed coming to work. During our meal, Sal walked from table to table, talking to all the diners. We chatted a few minutes and my husband and Sal, both from New Jersey, talked about things they had in common.

The second time we went to Sal's, he paused from tossing pizza dough. "Hey, New Jersey!" He called out. With all the customers coming through his door, I thought it was great that Sal not only remembered us, but that he remembered something about us.

Since that second visit, we have become regulars at Sal's. It meant a lot that he took the time to get to know us and build a relationship. The hostess also knows us. If she hasn't seen us in a while, she will ask how we've been. Our usual server remembers what we like to drink and what we normally order. Order something different? She's likely to say, "Not going with the usual tonight?" Everyone at Sal's makes us feel like we are part of their family.

Building relationships is important in any business. Taking the time to get to know your customers is the giant first step to building relationships. After all, we do want to go where everybody knows our names and they're always glad we came. When you welcome customers into your business and treat them like family, they'll become like family—loyal to you.

H O W   D O   I   M E A S U R E   U P ?

1. In my place of employment, what are the answers to:

    a. Who are my customers?

    _____

    _____

    b. What do they expect from our business?

    _____

    _____

    c. How do our products and services enhance their lives?

    _____

    _____

    d. How can I use these answers to establish a rapport with my customers?

    _____

    _____

2. What can I do to make sure I interact positively with all my customers?

    _____

    _____

3. How well do I ask questions to identify what my customers need? How well do I summarize what the customer said and then offer the best solution? How can I improve?

    _____

    _____

4. What do I do to show my customers I value them? How can I improve my skills?

    _____

    _____

5. How can I get to know new customers better? What can I do to strengthen relationships with our repeat customers?

    _____

    _____

6. Have I become familiar with the material about different types of customers in order to feel comfortable handling each of my customers? (If the answer is no, I need to review that section until I know the material.)

    _____

    _____

PART TWO

PUTTING YOUR CUSTOMERS FIRST

CHAPTER 4

Seeing Eye to Eye:
Face-to-Face Contacts

**CUSTOMERS MAY COME INTO A BUSINESS
BECAUSE OF THE PRODUCTS
BUT THEY WILL DECIDE TO COME AGAIN
ONLY WHEN THEY ARE TREATED WELL**

Write down a typical customer contact that is reflective of your face-to-face interactions:

_____

_____

_____

_____

_____

Think about this scenario as you work through this chapter. Use it as the example when answering the Practice Lesson questions at the end of the chapter.

Giving exceptional customer service, when dealing with customers in person, seems pretty simple on face value. Why, then, do so many of our interactions with customer service employees leave us feeling empty and unsatisfied?

Customers have been conditioned not to expect much, yet they deserve good service. When you treat customers as if they are important guests invited into your home, you show that you value them. When you treat customers as if they matter to you, they will feel appreciated.

CUSTOMER SERVICE IS FACE-TO-FACE CONTACTS

You have already learned that creating a positive first impression will help build the foundation for providing great customer service. Customers will judge your initial look, manner, and actions. Did you know that customers also get a first impression of your overall business when they come in? In addition to forming a first impression of you, your customers also judge your place of business by its look, image, and overall atmosphere.

Giving exceptional face-to-face customer service begins when your customers enter your place of business. From the moment a customer walks through your door, you have the opportunity to offer a warm and inviting welcome. That welcome includes what you say and what your customer sees. Helping the customer by showing him or her where to find items, answering questions, finding the right solution, and making sure he or she is satisfied before leaving will make all your customers feel appreciated and valued.

Their assessment, particularly when they are forming that crucial first impression, includes how you look and act, how your business looks and feels, and how well you interact with them. Customers may come to your business for a product or service, but they will decide to stay or leave based on an overall feeling of warmth or coolness.

Think about some businesses you went into recently. What was your first impression of them? Did you notice that some of them seemed to invite you inside with warmth, while others felt so chilly you could not wait to leave? In the businesses that made you feel welcome:

- *What did the employees do that made you feel welcome?*

- *What aspects of the business' appearance made you feel welcome?*

In the businesses that made you feel uncomfortable:

- *What did the employees do that made you feel uncomfortable?*

- *What aspects of the business' appearance made you feel uncomfortable?*

Next, think about the image your place of business presents to your customers. Mentally walk through your business from a customer's viewpoint. Start by walking through the front door. Take a good look at what your customers see.

Envision your business as if you are seeing it for the first time. Look at the colors, decorations, cleanliness, and neatness.

- *What do your customers see when they first step into your business?*

- *How easy is it to move about?*

- *How accessible are your display areas?*

- *Is the traffic flow pattern sensible?*

- *Is the lighting sufficient?*

- *Is everything clean, including bathrooms?*

Pay close attention to all details—your customers will. With your associates, try to come up with ideas to improve the overall look and image of your business. Think about color, function, and feel. Here are some things to pay attention to:

- Try to create a focal point for customers when they enter your business, whether it's an interesting piece of furniture, a piece of artwork, or an interesting display case. Create something that is memorable.

- Decorate your business in a style that suits the image you are trying to project. Knowing who your customers are is important when creating the appropriate look and feel.

- Pay close attention to cleanliness and organization. Even if your business is decorated to suit your customers, it will not hold their attention if they first see clutter or a dirty appearance.

- Remember, too, to focus on your own image. Think about the total package you present: your courtesy, attitude, appearance, manner of speaking, body language, listening skills, interest, and ability to build strong relationships.

PICTURE THIS...
THE WRONG WAY TO GIVE FACE-TO-FACE CUSTOMER SERVICE

Dave Benjamin had an appointment for a physical examination. He arrived at the physician's office, feeling slightly uneasy because it was his first appointment with this doctor. He walked into the office, looked around at the bland beige walls, row of uncomfortable-looking chairs, table with ripped magazines strewn about, and drab brown carpeting. Two other people were waiting. He eyed a wall and sliding window with a note taped on it: Sign in, and we'll call you when we're ready for you. He signed his name on the pad and took a seat. Someone on the other side of the window slid the window open, looked at his name, and quickly shut the window without saying a word. He sat, anxiously waiting and wondered when his name would be called.

The window slid open again. "Mr. Benjamin?"

Dave sprang up and walked quickly to the window.

"You need to fill out this form since you haven't been here before," a woman said, no expression in her voice. "When you're done, ring the bell."

Dave completed the paperwork, rang the bell, and sat back down. The woman slid the window open, took the paper, and then shut the window.

After the other two people were called, Dave waited for what seemed an eternity. A nurse finally called his name. "Mr. Benjamin?" He walked toward her. "Follow me. I need to weigh you and take your blood pressure."

What Went Wrong?

Presenting a positive business personality would have meant a lot to Dave. Bland beige walls, a row of uncomfortable-looking chairs, a table with ripped magazines, drab brown carpeting, and employees behind a glass wall sent a negative message about the office environment. The employee who sat behind the wall also sent a negative message that she was not approachable. Neither she nor the nurse made Dave feel welcome.

How Did the Customer Feel?

Dave formed a poor first impression. He felt uncomfortable walking into this office in the first place because this was his first visit and he did not know what to expect. When he walked into the waiting area, he felt that the doctor and the employees were not concerned about the way the office looked. When the receptionist handed him the form without saying hello, he felt even more uncomfortable. And finally, when the nurse came for him, she did nothing to put him at ease.

Remember that a customer's first impression is based on both the employees and the overall atmosphere of the company. A company can have a messy appearance and great employees. Likewise, a company may have a great appearance and employees with terrible attitudes. It pays off when you have both: a pleasant business appearance and caring employees.

Learn the following and you will be on your way to providing exceptional face-to-face customer service:

Step 1: Saying Hello: Greeting the Customer

Step 2: Between Hello and Goodbye: Helping the Customer

Step 3: Saying Goodbye: Ending the Interaction

In Dave's situation, his discomfort would have been eased if he walked into a clean, well-decorated, and organized waiting room. He would have felt much better if the receptionist talked to him. When the nurse came for him, she could have smiled and made small talk to make him feel comfortable.

STEP 1
SAYING HELLO: GREETING THE CUSTOMER

In Chapter 1 you learned how to make a good overall first impression, but there will be occasions when, no matter how hard you try, you cannot accomplish this. You might remind a customer of her old boyfriend. You might remind a customer of his rude neighbor. A customer might not like the way you look for no rational reason. When this happens, your first words will go a long way to begin building your customer service foundation.

Greet Every Customer

A quick smile, an interested look, and a friendly greeting will show your customers that you are genuinely happy they chose your business. A friendly greeting will help overcome any negative vibes that customers may pick up when they are forming their first impressions.

Make an Impressionable Opening Statement

What you say is important in presenting yourself well to your customers. When you greet them, say more than hello. Add something to let them know you are happy they walked through your door. Try something like: "Hi, welcome to Karen's Bakery," or "Good morning. We're glad you came in." When you say more than hello, you send the message to customers that you are interested in them and appreciate their choosing your business. If you remember a customer from a previous visit, acknowledge him or her differently. Say, for example, "Hello. It's great to see you again." Address him or her by name if you know it: "Hi Juanita, how are you doing today?"

Ask or Explain How You Can Provide Help and Give Your Name

After greeting your customers and making an impressionable opening statement, ask how you can help. Even if you work in an establishment where your customers come in to browse, let them know you are there if they need your assistance. You might say, "Are you looking for anything particular today?" or "My name is Jody and I'll be happy to help you in any way." In the doctor's office, the receptionist could have assured Dave she would help if he had any questions about the form he was asked to fill out. Since this was his first visit, talking to him, explaining the process, and asking if he had any questions would have put him at ease.

Tune In to Your Customers

Pay close attention to customers' body language. Watch for cues. Make eye contact and smile at them. Watch to see if they quickly and easily smile back. If not, try to pick up on emotional clues. Pay attention to their attitudes. When you are interested in your customers, you will be able to pick up on their moods and emotions, and you can respond accordingly. It was probably fairly evident that Dave was uncomfortable. Had the receptionist tuned in to Dave's actions and demeanor, she would have picked up valuable clues and could have said something positive to ease his discomfort.

PICTURE THIS...

THE RIGHT WAY TO GREET CUSTOMERS

Dave Benjamin arrived at the physician's office, feeling slightly uneasy because it was his first appointment with this doctor. He walked into the office, looked around at warm gold walls, an interesting grouping of chairs, a table with magazines neatly organized, and an Oriental rug covering the wood floors.

He saw an open sliding window. A cheerful woman smiled and greeted him. "Good morning, how are you today?"

"I'm fine, thank you. I'm Dave Benjamin. I have an appointment with Dr. Gilbert."

"Thank you, Mr. Benjamin. Since this is your first time seeing Dr. Gilbert, will you please complete this new patient information form?" She reviewed the form with Dave. "When you complete it, you can bring it back to me. My name is Kathy, and if you have any questions I'll be happy to help you." Sensing his discomfort, she smiled warmly.

Dave completed the form and returned it to Kathy.

She quickly looked it over. "Thanks, Mr. Benjamin. Have a seat, and Dr. Gilbert's nurse will call you. It shouldn't take long."

How Did the Customer Feel?

When Kathy warmly greeted Dave, she gave him her full attention. She projected a confident, caring attitude that made Dave feel she was interested in him. Tuning in to his feelings, Kathy sensed he felt uneasy, so she made it a point of offering to help him in any way she could and assuring him he would not have to wait long. Dave's first impression was positive and he felt less tense.

STEP 2
BETWEEN HELLO AND GOODBYE: HELPING THE CUSTOMER

After greeting your customers, it is time to get to the nuts and bolts of helping them. They came to you for a reason. Finding out that reason and finding the best solution is your next step.

Pay attention to that one customer—and only that one customer. Show you are interested in helping by listening actively and making eye contact. Remember the employee at the deli who handled the contact the wrong way in Chapter 2? When he was helping Steve, he kept looking to the door whenever someone came in. When you are helping a customer, stay focused and tuned in. Looking at other people sends a clear message that those people are more important than your customer.

TIP

> If a phone call comes in while you are helping a customer, ask the caller to hold while you finish or offer to call back. Never make the customer, who is ready to do business, wait while you take a call.

Show and Tell

When a customer asks where something is located, show him or her rather than pointing or telling where it is. Walk the customer to that area of the store. If it is a small item, pick it up and hand it to the customer. If a customer asks about a product, tell him or her about it, offering a good description.

Make the Most of Your Question-and-Answer Period

Refer back to Chapter 2, Step 4, and Chapter 3, Step 3. If the customer asks for a specific item, show the item to him or her and then ask questions to make sure it is the best product for the purpose. Use a combination of open and closed questions to learn more about the customer's needs. Make a recommendation based on what he or she tells you.

Know When to Stay and When to Go

Pick up on your customer's cues to determine whether you should stay and help or whether he or she wants to be left alone. Sometimes people come in just to browse; other times, they may be unsure about what solution they are looking for. Do not be overbearing. If they want time to look around, say, "I'll be right here if I can help you," or "I'll be happy to help if you need anything."

Effectiveness and Efficiency Are Important

Being effective means finding the right solution for your customer's needs, and the only way you can do that is to know your products and services. Learn all you can about what your business has to offer. If you are unsure about a customer's needs, ask your manager or a coworker to help find the right product or service. Being efficient means finding the best solution quickly. You can be knowledgeable, but if you take too long to come up with a recommendation or find a solution, you are going to lose ground with your customers. Customers value employees who are both effective and efficient.

BRAINSTORM

What steps should you take to help customers? Discuss these steps with your manager or instructor. Refer to the contact you wrote down on the first page of this chapter. Discuss this and other types of customer contacts you normally handle. It is important that you understand the basic steps for assisting your customers. Remember, though, that one size does not fit all. Flexibility is important when dealing with different types of customers and scenarios. That is the only sure way you can give each customer individualized service.

PICTURE THIS...
THE RIGHT WAY TO HELP CUSTOMERS

Soon a nurse came into the waiting room. "Mr. Benjamin?" Dave walked toward her. She said, "My name is Ann. How are you doing?"

"I'm fine, thanks."

"Great. Come with me. I'll get you weighed and take your blood pressure first. Then Dr. Gilbert will see you."

How Did the Customer Feel?

By the time Ann came for him, Dave felt comfortable in Dr. Gilbert's office. Both Kathy and Ann explained the procedures to Dave. Because Dave was comfortable with the employees, with the look of the office, and with the organized manner in which it was run, Dave felt he was in good hands.

STEP 3
SAYING GOODBYE: ENDING THE INTERACTION

Customers are going to remember something about their visit to your company. Whether they do business with you or not, why not make their visit memorable by making them feel valued?

Find the Right Solution

When you find the right solution, your customers will feel good about coming to you for help. Sometimes you may not have any solution to offer, but even when you are unable to give them what they need, show them that you tried your best.

Make Sure the Customer Is Satisfied

When you have asked the right questions and received the correct answers, when you have identified the customer's needs, and when you have found the best solution, then go one step further to make sure the customer is satisfied. If you know the customer is happy, validate his or her decision by adding an assurance, "I'm sure you'll be happy with that choice. It's one of our most popular items." If you feel the customer may be hesitant or unsure, ask something like, "Do you have any questions about how this works?" If you were unable to find the right solution, apologize and say, "I'm sorry we didn't have the _____ you were looking for." As for the browsing customer who is leaving without doing business, you might want to ask, "Is there anything I can help you with today?"

Acknowledge Customers for Coming In to Your Business

Always let your customers know that you appreciate their business by saying something such as, "Enjoy your new. . . ." or "I'm glad I could resolve your billing problem." If he or she does not do business with you, say, "Thanks for coming in," or "Thanks. Next time I hope we have what you're looking for." Let your customers know you hope to see them again by saying, "Please come back soon."

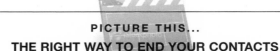

PICTURE THIS...
THE RIGHT WAY TO END YOUR CONTACTS

Dr. Gilbert completed Dave's physical. "Mr. Benjamin, it looks like you are taking great care of yourself. Do you have any questions?"

"I can't think of any."

"After you finish dressing, you can go to the reception area, and they'll finish your paperwork. Unless something changes and you need to come in, I'll see you in a year. It was great meeting you." Dr. Gilbert smiled, shook Dave's hand, and said goodbye.

Kathy saw him coming. "Done already? I have your paperwork right here. Do you have any questions?"

"No, Dr. Gilbert was great. She spent a lot of time with me. I'm glad I came to see her."

"That's nice to hear. Would you like us to mail you a reminder card for your next appointment?"

"No, that's OK. I'll remember to call."

"We do get booked up quickly, so please try to call about two months prior so we can get you a convenient appointment."

"Thanks for letting me know. I'll make sure I do that."

"Thank you for coming in and have a great day."

How Did the Customer Feel?

Kathy ended on a positive note by asking if Dave had any questions. His answer told her he was satisfied with his interaction with Dr. Gilbert. She ended by thanking him for coming in.

The following week, one of Dave's coworkers asked if anyone knew of a good doctor. "I do," Dave answered. "I just saw Dr. Gilbert last week for a physical. She was great. Besides that, the office is clean, the staff is very friendly, and they went out of their way to make me feel comfortable. I'd definitely recommend her."

Whenever you have your customer hat on and go into a business, pay close attention to the way you are treated. Think about the things you liked and the things you did not like. Learn from watching others. Make sure you treat customers the way you like to be treated.

PICTURE THIS...
PUTTING IT ALL TOGETHER

Dave Benjamin arrived at the physician's office feeling slightly uneasy because it was his first appointment with this doctor. He walked into the office, looked around at warm gold walls, an interesting grouping of chairs, a table with magazines neatly organized, and an Oriental rug covering the wood floors.

He saw an open sliding glass window. A cheerful woman smiled and greeted him. "Good morning, how are you today?"

"I'm fine, thank you. I'm Dave Benjamin. I have an appointment with Dr. Gilbert."

"Thank you, Mr. Benjamin. Since this is your first time seeing Dr. Gilbert, will you please complete this new patient information form?" She reviewed the form with Dave. "When you complete it, you can bring it back to me. My name is Kathy, and if you have any questions I'll be happy to help you." Sensing his discomfort, she smiled warmly.

Dave completed the form and returned it to Kathy.

She quickly looked it over. "Thanks, Mr. Benjamin. Have a seat, and Dr. Gilbert's nurse will call you. It shouldn't take long."

Soon a nurse came into the waiting room. "Mr. Benjamin?" Dave walked toward her. She said, "My name is Ann. How are you doing?"

"I'm fine, thanks."

"Great. Come with me. I'll get you weighed and take your blood pressure first. Then Dr. Gilbert will see you."

Dr. Gilbert completed Dave's physical. "Mr. Benjamin, it looks like you are taking great care of yourself. Do you have any questions?"

"I can't think of any."

"After you finish dressing, you can go to the reception area, and they'll finish your paperwork. Unless something changes and you need to come in, I'll see you in a year. It was great meeting you." Dr. Gilbert smiled, shook Dave's hand, and said goodbye.

Kathy saw him coming. "Done already? I have your paperwork right here. Do you have any questions?"

"No, Dr. Gilbert was great. She spent a lot of time with me. I'm glad I came to see her."

"That's nice to hear. Would you like us to mail you a reminder card for your next appointment?"

"No, that's OK. I'll remember to call."

"We do get booked up quickly, so please try to call about two months prior so we can get you a convenient appointment."

"Thanks for letting me know. I'll make sure I do that."

"Thank you for coming in and have a great day."

Although you may not automatically think of a physician's office as a customer service provider, think again. Every business provides customer service. It is important that anyone—in any business—who interacts with customers understands this. Customers, even patients, will go to someone else if they are not satisfied with their treatment.

Customers May Come Into a Business Because of the Products but They Will Decide to Come Again Only When They Are Treated Well

Consumer confidence has hit an all-time low. Let's face it: People have become more wary when it comes to business dealings. They are— and have the right to be—selective about where they spend their cash. Now is not the time to take your customers for granted. Treat them poorly? They will leave as fast as they came in. Not interested in finding a workable solution? They will find a business that is interested.

Getting customers into your brick and mortar business may be a little tougher in financially challenging times, but when customers do come in, make sure you do everything you can to hold on to them. It really isn't that difficult:

BUSINESS
NØT
AS USUAL

- Welcome your customers into your business. Immediately begin building a relationship by establishing a rapport.

- Find the best solution for each customer. Communicate effectively by asking questions, answering questions, and most importantly, listening carefully.

- End on a positive note. Use basic courtesies such as saying, "Thank you for coming in."

When you demonstrate to your customers that you want their business, you send a powerful message that you are going to do all you can to keep their business. When you do that, you increase your chances of staying in business.

- Smile and show enthusiasm both for your customers and for your job.

- Keep a friendly and helpful demeanor.

- Customers value effectiveness and efficiency—learn all you can and do it quickly.

K E Y   P O I N T S

Step 1: Saying Hello: Greeting the Customer

- Greet every customer.

- Make an impressionable opening statement.

- Ask or explain how you can help and give your name.

- Tune in to your customers.

Step 2: Between Hello and Goodbye: Helping the Customer

- Pay attention to the one customer.

- Show and tell.

- Make the most of your question-and-answer period.

- Know when to stay and when to go.

- Effectiveness and efficiency are important.

Step 3: Saying Goodbye: Ending the Interaction

- Find the right solution.

- Make sure the customer is satisfied.

- Acknowledge customers for coming into your business.

P R A C T I C E   L E S S O N

Refer to the customer contact example you noted at the beginning of the chapter.

Step 1: Saying Hello: Greeting the Customer

What will you do when customers come in?

_____

_____

Step 2: Between Hello and Goodbye: Helping the Customer

What are the general steps you are going to take to help your typical customer?

_____

_____

Step 3: Saying Goodbye: Ending the Interaction

What will you do before the customer leaves your business?

_____

_____

What will you say to a customer for whom you could not find the right solution?

_____

_____

_____

DOING IT RIGHT!

I bet if you asked one hundred people to list their favorite pastimes, not one would list grocery shopping among their top ten. It just happens to be one of those necessary tasks in life. We eat; therefore, we grocery shop.

Grocery store managers understand this fact. They know we will come. Why, then, should grocery stores care about customer service?

The truth is that many don't seem to care. You've probably been to stores where the parking lot is littered with shopping carts, employees bury themselves in their work, shelves are sometimes empty, the cashier grumbles a disinterested greeting, you have to bag your own groceries—or worse, get stuck with the bagger who throws the heavy items on top of the light ones. You leave the store with your groceries, but not with a positive feeling.

It's not that way at the grocery store where I shop. Providing exceptional customer service is their number one goal. Chip, the store manager, his department and assistant managers, and the employees actively demonstrate that they care about their customers.

Chip can usually be found not in his office, but walking around the store, pitching in to help when needed. His department and assistant managers are where they should be: in their respective departments, on the floor, always close at hand.

Chip and his management team take care of all the little details that add up to a positive shopping experience. Carts are rounded up frequently. If you need help, an employee is always nearby. Employees are constantly stocking shelves. The cashiers are friendly and will chat as they scan. And don't even think about bagging your own groceries. Every time I try, a manager sends someone right over—and the groceries are bagged correctly.

Customer service really begins with setting expectations—if Chip didn't care, his employees wouldn't. If he wasn't a hands-on manager, his department and assistant managers wouldn't be hands-on either. He sets high customer service expectations and, most importantly, because he walks the talk his employees walk the talk.

You see, even a chore such as grocery shopping can turn into a pleasant experience when the managers and employees genuinely care for their customers. When your customers have to do business with you—why not do what you can to make their experience pleasurable? Think about it this way: Doing everything you can to make your customers feel good makes you feel good. Knowing you did your best is always satisfying.

H O W   D O   I   M E A S U R E   U P ?

1. When I greet my customers do I show enthusiasm and interest? What standard greeting can I use for new customers? What can I say and do to welcome my customers?

    _____

    _____

    _____

2. How effective and efficient am I in helping customers? What technical skills do I need to learn? Do I always remember to show and tell and ask questions to make sure the customer finds the best solution? If not, what internal cues can I teach myself to do better?

    _____

    _____

    _____

3. Do I make sure all my customers are satisfied, whether or not they do business with us? How can I improve in this area?

    _____

    _____

    _____

Saying It with a Smile: Telephone Contacts

ALWAYS MAKE IT EASY FOR YOUR CUSTOMERS TO DO BUSINESS WITH YOU

Write down a typical exchange that you would have with a customer who contacts you by telephone:

_____

_____

_____

_____

_____

Think about the scenario you have created above as you work through this chapter. Use it as the example when answering the Practice Lesson questions at the end of the chapter.

If your job is to handle customer contacts by telephone, then you have probably figured out that this requires a different skill set than dealing with people face to face. Listening becomes even more important when you cannot see your customers. If you do not listen completely, it is impossible to pick up on the cues you get nonverbally when you can see the other person. You may miss out on important details. When customers cannot see you, what you say, how you say it, and what you do not say all are equally important.

CUSTOMER SERVICE IS TELEPHONE CONTACTS

Answering promptly and greeting your customers with enthusiasm and a willingness to help gets you off on the right foot. In addition, maintaining a professional and friendly telephone demeanor, assuring the customer you can help, keeping an ongoing dialogue, asking appropriate questions, and responding appropriately to your customers enables you to interact well with customers by phone.

Staying tuned in by verbalizing what you are doing is important. Silence, to a customer on the other end of a phone line, can create confusion: Are you still there? What are you doing? Let them know you are still there and working.

Before hanging up, recapping what you are going to do, asking if you can do anything more, and thanking customers for doing business with you leaves them with a good feeling about calling your place of business.

Think about some businesses you called recently. What was your impression of your phone exchanges?

In your phone contacts that were positive experiences, *what did the employee say and do that made you feel comfortable?*

In your phone contacts that were negative experiences, *what did the employee say and do that caused you to feel uncomfortable?*

Now think about your own place of business. Think about how you and your coworkers respond to customers when they call. Work through a mental phone call from start to finish and ask yourself the following questions:

- *Do you handle contacts in a manner that makes customers feel good about calling your company?*

- *When you answer calls, how do you greet customers and welcome them "into" your business?*

- *What do you say to assure customers you will help them?*

- *While you are handling phone requests, what do you say or ask to make your customers comfortable?*

- *If you called your company, how would you feel?*

Focus on all aspects of the phone contact, because your customers are going to. As a group, discuss ways in which you can make your phone customers feel as though they are walking through your door rather than calling you. Finding ways to make them feel welcome is your main goal in this exercise.

PICTURE THIS...
THE WRONG WAY TO HANDLE TELEPHONE CONTACTS

Diane Parker likes the convenience of shopping by catalog. She sometimes orders over the Internet, but prefers calling because she likes interacting with a person. Ashley works in a catalog call center, where her job is to take orders from customers. When she received a call from Diane, the interaction went like this:

"VeeJay's Sportswear."

"Hi, I'd like to place a catalog order."

"May I have your name and billing address?"

"Yes, Diane Parker. My address is 23 Sycamore Road. . . ."

"Is that the address to which you want your order shipped?"

"Yes."

"What is your first catalog number?"

"14236."

"Size?"

"Medium."

"Color?"

"Rose."

"Next item?"

Diane continued to give her list of items, along with her credit card information. Then there was silence on the other end of the line. Diane waited. And waited. She began to wonder what was happening. Did the employee put her on hold? Had she forgotten about her? Had she taken a break? "Hello," she said into the silence.

"I'm here," came a bland reply. "I'm waiting for your order to process. It shouldn't be long."

Diane waited again.

"Your order has gone through. All items are in stock and will be shipped out tomorrow. Is there anything else I can help you with?"

"No thanks."

"Thank you for calling."

Diane hung up, hoping the employee got all the items correct.

What Went Wrong?

Ashley was efficient in taking Diane's order. She most likely followed her company's instructions as to how catalog orders should be taken. But it sounded as though Diane was giving her order to an automated system. Ashley added nothing to her contact with Diane. Sophisticated call answering equipment could have input the order just as well. While Ashley may have handled the order process correctly, she left out the important detail of putting a personal touch into the contact. It is this personal touch in your phone conversations that will make you, as well as your company, come alive in an interaction with a customer.

How Did the Customer Feel?

Because Ashley did nothing to establish a rapport, Diane did not feel comfortable with their interaction. Then when Ashley did not recap the order, Diane wondered if she input all the items correctly. Diane did not have a warm feeling about this company.

When you deal with customers on the telephone, your verbal communication skills, particularly the tone of your voice, are important. Your customers will only "see" you through your voice. So whether your attitude is tinged with enthusiasm, sarcasm, boredom, or disinterest, your customers will hear you—loudly and clearly. Make sure the attitude you convey is that you are enthusiastic about helping them.

Learn the following steps and you will give exceptional customer service to your telephone customers.

Step 1: Putting Your Best Ear Forward

Step 2: Saying Hello: The Opener

Step 3: Between Hello and Goodbye: Helping the Customer

Step 4: Saying Goodbye: The Closer

In Diane's phone call, Ashley could have shown more enthusiasm by answering the call, "Thank you for calling VeeJay's. How can I help you today?" She could have interacted more throughout the contact. For example, she could have repeated the item name when Diane gave the number: "Item 14236, the denim jacket. What size and color would you like that in?" Small verbalizations like these can make a big difference with customers.

STEP 1
PUTTING YOUR BEST EAR FORWARD: LISTENING CAREFULLY

When you communicate with another person face to face, you may be able to fudge when you do not listen completely. You can pick up cues by paying attention to a person's body language. You may even be able to drift off and still pick up somewhere in the middle of the conversation by going with the flow and observing the other person's actions as he or she speaks. This is not so when you are on the phone. When you cannot see the other person, your only means of communication is the give and take of listening and talking. When you do not listen effectively, it can be pretty tough to respond effectively. When you handle customers by telephone, listening is critical.

Review Chapter 2, Step 6: Focus entirely on your customer; listen completely; and remain objective—do not judge. If you follow this approach when dealing with a customer over the phone, you will be able to "hear" their attitude by listening carefully to the tone of his or her voice.

Listen to the Customer's Opening Statement

The first words out of the customer's mouth tell you the reason for the call. Never let the first words out of your mouth be to ask your customer to repeat his or her opening statement because you were not giving your full attention.

Write Down or Input Key Points

Have pen and paper ready or have the correct computer screen displayed when you take a call. If the customer gives you his or her name, write it down. If the customer seems upset, write down the main points of the opening statement. For example, *Mrs. Brennan—received wrong color jacket—got blue, wanted white.* You do not have to write verbatim, just highlight the key points.

Listen Without Interrupting

If Mrs. Brennan is telling you why she is calling and you interrupt her midsentence, she is not going to be very happy: "This is Mrs. Brennan. I just received my order and one of the items. . . ." "Hold on just a second Mrs. Brennan, I'm finishing up an order. As soon as my screen clears, I'll be able to help you." If Mrs. Brennan was not upset when she called, she most likely would be if an employee interrupted her and was not ready to help. Even if the computer screen needed to clear, the employee could have listened and jotted down the key points.

Give the Customer You Are Helping Your Full Attention

If you don't pay attention, your phone conversation is liable to go as follows: "This is Mrs. Brennan. I just received my order and one of the items isn't what I ordered." "What is your name?" "Mrs. Brennan." "You said you received an order?" Because this employee did not pay attention, Mrs. Brennan is going to have to repeat herself. How do you think she will feel when she does? When you pay attention and listen to the reason for the call, you can begin finding the best solution for that customer.

STEP 2
SAYING HELLO: THE OPENER

Now that we reviewed the importance of listening, starting with the customer's opening statement, we can begin the call process.

Answer on the First Ring

Customers expect a business line to be answered on the first, and no later than the second, ring. After that, they may hang up and you will have lost a potential customer.

Give the Name of Your Business, Your Name, and Then an Opening Statement or Question

When giving your opening statement or question, sound enthusiastic and ready to help. Speak in a professional, yet friendly, tone. With practice, you can manage the balance between sounding mechanical or overly friendly. It helps to speak in a natural voice, without forcing an unnatural tone.

TIP

> When speaking to a customer on the phone, never chew gum or eat. You might think the person on the other end does not hear it, but you may be wrong.

Assure the Customer You Can Help

Listen closely to your customer's opening statement and respond accordingly. For instance, you might say something like, "Absolutely. I can help you with that." In situations where you are going to refer the customer to another department or employee, offer some assurance that his or her call won't be disconnected. For example, "I'm going to transfer you to the department that can take care of this for you, but I will stay on the line until someone answers."

Work on Relationship Building from the Beginning of the Contact

Make a good first impression by speaking in an upbeat tone that conveys a willingness to help. Establish a rapport by finding common ground. Address the customer by name if you know it.

TIP

> It is generally all right to use the customer's first name if that is how he or she identified him- or herself. Use good judgment and when in doubt, address the customer using Mr., Mrs. (if the customer has identified herself in that manner), or Ms. plus their last name. Let the customer be the one to let you know if it is all right to use a first name.

THE RIGHT WAY TO BEGIN TELEPHONE CONTACTS

"Thank you for calling VeeJay's Sportswear. My name is Ashley. How may I help you today?"

How Did the Customer Feel?

Ashley answered the call on the first ring. She gave the name of the business, her name, and asked how she could help. Diane picked up on Ashley's enthusiasm and willingness to be of assistance.

STEP 3

BETWEEN HELLO AND GOODBYE: HELPING THE CUSTOMER

Between hello and goodbye, you have the opportunity to handle your customer's request in a manner that leaves him or her feeling good about calling your company or that leaves the customer wondering why he or she bothered calling. You are your company's voice; how you handle your customer's request by telephone is how the customer is going to remember your company. Be sure you represent it well.

Summarize the Customer's Opening Statement

Before you attempt to handle a customer's request, make sure you understand what he or she wants. Recap what the customer said without repeating it verbatim. In Mrs. Brennan's call, you could say, "You received your order, but we sent you a blue jacket instead of white?" This way, the customer will clear up any confusion before you go on: "No, I received a white jacket but I wanted blue." When possible, incorporate the summary into your assurance statement: "I'll be happy to take your catalog order."

Verbalize What You Are Doing

Explain to your customer what you are doing throughout the contact. Never assume the person on the other end understands. During silences, the customer may be wondering if you are still there. If you need to ask a series of questions, explain what you will be doing so the customer does not think you are interrogating, "Mrs. Brennan, I'm going to need some additional information to help you. Do you have your invoice handy?" Now when you begin asking questions, Mrs. Brennan understands what you are doing.

TIP

If you are a new employee, it is all right to say so. Doing so may help you build a rapport with your customers. Everyone has been new at a job, and customers will relate and be patient with you. You can say something like, "I really appreciate your patience. I'm new and I want to make sure I input everything correctly for you."

Put Your Personal Touch Into the Contact

You can maintain professionalism and still show your human side. Talk to the customer while you are waiting for a computer screen to change: "It'll be just a moment for the next screen. How are you doing today?" If a customer asks you to do something you are unsure of, say so. Then, if necessary, follow up with, "I'll check with my supervisor. I want to make sure I handle this correctly."

Before a Lengthy Pause,
Tell the Customer What Is Happening

There are many instances in which you will need to pause in your conversation with a customer. For example, you might need to wait for the order to process, wait for another computer screen to come up, or read notes from previous contacts. You may be a new employee and not yet working up to speed. Let the customer know why there is a pause in your conversation. This will avoid awkward silences. You can say, "It'll take a moment for the order to process. Then I can give you a confirmation number. I'll stay on the line with you, though."

When Putting Customers on Hold, Explain Why

Explaining why you are going to put a customer on hold is a common courtesy that will be appreciated: "Mrs. Brennan, I'm going to put you on hold so I can see what happened with your order." In addition, be sure to tell your customer approximately how long it will take: "It may take me a few minutes to get the information I need to help you." If you put a customer on hold and then find it is taking longer than you thought, return to the line and offer an update: "Mr. Perkins, I'm still waiting for my technician to give me an answer. It shouldn't take that much longer." If the wait time will be extremely long, offer to call the customer back. Always make a specific commitment: "I'll get back to you by five o'clock today with the information," rather than "I'll call you back as soon as possible." As soon as possible may mean one time frame to you, but an entirely different time frame to your customers.

BRAINSTORM

Your job may require that you make outgoing phone contacts or cold calls for sales. As a group, create an outline for handling these types of calls. Include the following aspects of your contact in your script:

- Greeting—introducing yourself and your company.

- Explaining the reason for your call.

- Questions you will ask.

Role play to practice your message before making outgoing calls. And remember that this "script" is a framework only. Flexibility helps you put your personality into the conversation.

THE RIGHT WAY TO HELP TELEPHONE CUSTOMERS

"Hi, I'd like to place a catalog order."

"I'll be glad to take your order. May I have your name and your billing address?"

"Sure. It's Diane Parker. My address is 23 Sycamore Road. . . ."

"Is that the address to which you want your order shipped?"

"Yes."

"It'll take just a minute for my screen to change. How are you doing today?"

"I'm great, how are you?"

"I'm doing great, too. Hmm, our system seems to be a little slow this morning, but the screen should come right up." After a short pause, Ashley said, "Here we go. I'm ready to take your order now. What is your first catalog number?"

"SU—14236."

"That's the misses denim jacket. What size and color would you like that?"

"Size medium in rose."

"I have the same jacket, and it's really comfortable. What is the next item number?"

"SU—14707."

"Denim slacks. Size and color?"

"Size ten in rose."

"All right. Next?"

Ashley input all the information, adding a personal touch from time to time until Diane finished.

"Thank you. It'll take a moment for the order to process and then I'll give you your confirmation number."

How Did the Customer Feel?

Diane felt comfortable during the phone call. Ashley assured her she could help, summarized the reason for the call, and verbalized what she was doing throughout the contact. Before pauses, Ashley explained the reason for the delay. She built a relationship throughout the exchange by being friendly, yet professional and that came across to Diane.

STEP 4
SAYING GOODBYE: THE CLOSER

Learning how to effectively handle customer contacts by telephone begins when you answer the call, continues when you take care of the customer's request, and ends when you say goodbye. Remember, telephone customers are going to judge your company by their interactions with you. Ending the call effectively will make them feel good about their choice.

Recap What You Are Going to Do

When you have finished handling the customer's request, end the contact on a positive note by assuring him or her that you either have or will handle the request. Say something like, "Mr. Downs, I have issued a credit for the finance charge." In the case of a lengthy request, it is not necessary to recap each item. You could say, "Mr. Downs, I've issued a credit and noted your account of the other items we discussed."

Gain the Customer's Acceptance

When you recap, the customer knows exactly what you will be doing to assist him or her. Wait for an acknowledgment and acceptance to make sure the customer agrees with your plans. If there is a mistake in your recap, the customer will let you know. Doing this will cut down on errors and will ultimately increase customer satisfaction.

Ask If You Can Help with Anything Else

This is another way to show your human touch, as well as a nice way to end the contact. Asking if you can help with anything else gives your customers a chance to pause and think before hanging up. They will appreciate the memory jogger.

Give Your Name Again

Let the customer know you will be happy to help if he or she needs to call back. For example, you might say, "My name is Kevin, and if you need anything else I'll be glad to help you with it." If you work in a large call center that would make it difficult for the customer to reach you personally, you can say: "My name is Kevin. Your order has been processed. I'll give you the confirmation number as soon as it comes up. If you need to call back anyone can access your order either by the confirmation number or by your name and address."

Thank the Customer for Calling Your Business

Always end on a positive note: "Thank you for calling (name) Company. Have a great day."

PICTURE THIS...
THE RIGHT WAY TO END TELEPHONE CONTACTS

After a short pause, Ashley said, "Mrs. Parker, your order for the five items has been processed. Everything is in stock and will be shipped out tomorrow. Do you have a pen and paper handy so I can give you your confirmation number?"

"Yes."

"The number is 061524."

"OK. Great."

"Is there anything else I can help you with today?"

"No, I think that should do it."

"Again, my name is Ashley. If you need to call back regarding your order anyone here can reference it by the confirmation number or by your name and address. Thank you for calling VeeJay's and have a great day."

"Thank you."

How Did the Customer Feel?

Diane was glad that Ashley recapped the total number of items in her order. By asking if she could help with anything else, Diane had the opportunity to think and respond. Diane appreciated that Ashley gave her name and thanked her for calling, and felt good about contacting this company.

When you call a company as a customer, pay close attention to the way you are treated. Analyze the steps that went well and those that did not. You can learn from thinking about the way you want to be treated as a customer, and then treat your customers in that manner.

PICTURE THIS...
PUTTING IT ALL TOGETHER

"Thank you for calling VeeJay's Sportswear. My name is Ashley. How may I help you today?"

"Hi, I'd like to place a catalog order."

"I'll be glad to take your order. May I have your name and your billing address?"

"Sure. It's Diane Parker. My address is 23 Sycamore Road. . . ."

"Is that the address to which you want your order shipped?"

"Yes."

"It'll take just a minute for my screen to change. How are you doing today?"

"I'm great, how are you?"

"I'm doing great, too. Hmm, our system seems to be a little slow this morning, but the screen should come right up." After a short pause, Ashley said, "Here we go. I'm ready to take your order now. What is your first catalog number?"

"SU—14236."

"That's the misses denim jacket. What size and color would you like that?"

"Size medium in rose."

"I have the same jacket, and it's really comfortable. What is the next item number?"

"SU—14707."

"Denim slacks. Size and color?"

"Size ten in rose."

"All right. Next?"

Ashley input all the information, adding a personal touch from time to time until Diane finished.

"Thank you. It'll take a moment for the order to process and then I'll give you your confirmation number."

After a short pause, Ashley said, "Mrs. Parker, your order for the five items has been processed. Everything is in stock and will be shipped out tomorrow. Do you have a pen and paper handy so I can give you your confirmation number?"

"Yes."

"The number is 061524."

"OK. Great."

"Is there anything else I can help you with today?"

"No, I think that should do it."

"Again, my name is Ashley. If you need to call back regarding your order anyone here can reference it by the confirmation number or by your name and address. Thank you for calling VeeJay's and have a great day."

"Thank you."

The right combination to satisfying customers by telephone is to answer promptly, display a genuine willingness to help, know what to do, do it right, and do it with enthusiasm.

BUSINESS NØT AS USUAL

Always Make It Easy for Your Customers to Do Business with You

Competition is greater when you conduct business by phone. Customers have national, and in some cases even global, options. Your phone customers may be your primary means of doing business, but even if they aren't, you should always give them the same level of service as your walk-in customers.

What customers want most when they call a business is easy access and a helpful voice. When you answer with enthusiasm on the first ring and follow through by handling calls effectively and efficiently, you are off to a good start in satisfying your phone customers. If you have an automated system, make it quick, easy, and painless for them and always offer an option to speak to an employee.

Perhaps your phone isn't ringing as often lately. When it does ring, do everything you can to make your phone customers feel welcome, comfortable, and ultimately happy that they called your place of business. When your number one goal is to make it easy for your customers to do business with you, you increase the likelihood that your phone is going to continue to ring. So remember:

- Establish your credibility by assuring your customer you can help.

- Your attitude comes through the phone lines; make yours a positive one.

- Smile; your customer will "hear" your smile through your voice.

- Give the customer your full attention.

- Build rapport throughout the contact by talking to your customer.

- Always thank your customer for calling the business.

K E Y   P O I N T S

Step 1: Putting Your Best Ear Forward

- Listen to the customer's opening statement.

- Write down or input key points.

- Listen without interrupting.

- Give the customer you are helping your full attention.

Step 2: Saying Hello: The Opener

- Answer on the first ring.

- Give the name of your business, your name, and an opening statement or question.

- Assure the customer you can help.

- Work on relationship building from the beginning of the contact.

Step 3: Between Hello and Goodbye: Helping the Customer

- Summarize the customer's opening statement.

- Verbalize what you are doing.

- Put your personal touch into the contact.

- Before a lengthy pause, tell the customer what is happening.

- When putting customers on hold, explain why.

Step 4: Saying Goodbye: The Closer

- Recap what you are going to do.

- Gain the customer's acceptance.

- Ask if you can help with anything else.

- Give your name again.

- Thank the customer for calling your business.

P R A C T I C E   L E S S O N

Step 1: Putting Your Best Ear Forward

Write down some things you can do to be a better listener on the telephone.

_____

_____

Refer to the customer contact example you noted at the beginning of the chapter.

Step 2: Saying Hello: The Opener

Write down how you will greet your customer.

_____

_____

Step 3: Between Hello and Goodbye: Helping the Customer

Assure the customer you can help. Summarize the customer's opening statement.

_____

_____

What are some ways you can verbalize what you are doing?

_____

_____

Write down what you might say when there is a pause. Write down what you might say before putting a customer on hold.

_____

_____

Step 4: Saying Goodbye: The Closer

Recap how you are going to handle the customer's request.

_____

_____

How will you end the contact? (Remember to ask if you can help with anything else, give your name again, and thank the customer for calling your business.)

_____

_____

_____

DOING IT RIGHT

A while back I received an e-mail ad for a book manufacturing company. I was unfamiliar with this company, but occasionally I need books printed so I saved the e-mail. Later, when I was working on a manuscript for a client, I reread the e-mail and phoned the company for a job estimate. Rick answered the phone in a professional, helpful manner. After he enthusiastically assured me he could help, I felt I was off to a good start.

Rick completed his paperwork, and then e-mailed me a proposal for my job. Everything looked good—on the surface. I still had doubts, though. I had never done business with this company. They were located far from me, so I had not seen their building. Nor had I received a recommendation from a business associate. I hadn't even heard of them until they sent me that e-mail ad. How could I trust them when I didn't know anything about them?

That's exactly what I asked Rick. "Everything in your proposal looks great," I said, "but I don't know anything about your company. We haven't established a business relationship. Why should I do business with you when I don't really know who you are and what the outcome is going to be?"

I loved his answer: "We pride ourselves on giving each of our customers the best possible service. We understand it's all about trust. Believe me, I am going to do everything in my power to earn your trust and confidence in me. I will not let you down."

Then he added, "Besides, we're here to stay in business. We know the only way we're going to do that is through our customers."

I decided to go with this company because of Rick's confident assurance. I completed the necessary paperwork and trusted him to do the right thing. Surprisingly, he not only did the right thing by producing a good product, he did it sooner than the expected due date, which not only thrilled my client, but more than thrilled me.

I called Rick to thank him and to tell him that he did exactly what he said he'd do: earn my trust. I pressed him further on how he beat his completion estimate.

Because I'm in the customer service business, he shared his company's secret. "We have two deadlines: an external one that we give customers, and an internal deadline that we give ourselves. Almost always, we're able to meet our internal deadline, which we know is going to make our customers happy."

Think about that: here is a small business that figured out a unique way to stand out. When you conduct business by phone, you not only need to earn your customers' trust, but you need to do something special to stand out in their minds. That something special is giving outstanding service.

When customers who don't know you are willing to give you their blind trust to do the right thing for them, make it your top priority never to let them down.

H O W   D O   I   M E A S U R E   U P ?

1. How well do I listen to my phone customers? What do I do to shut out distractions so that I pay complete attention? What can I do better?

_____

_____

_____

2. What do I say to welcome customers? What do I do to make them feel comfortable about calling our company?

_____

_____

_____

3. When I am helping customers, do I remember to summarize their opening statement? Do I remember to verbalize what I am doing, especially during pauses and when placing customers on hold? What can I do to improve these telephone skills?

_____

_____

_____

4. Before hanging up, do I recap the customers' requests and gain their acceptance? How do I know if each customer is satisfied before ending the call? How can I improve?

_____

_____

_____

6

Looking Before You Leap: E-Customer Contacts

**GIVE YOUR E-CUSTOMERS THE SAME QUALITY
OF SERVICE YOU GIVE YOUR FACE-TO-FACE
AND TELEPHONE CUSTOMERS**

Write down a typical customer contact that is reflective of your E-commerce interactions:

_____

_____

_____

_____

_____

Think about the scenario you created above as you work through this chapter. Use it as the example when answering the Practice Lesson questions at the end of the chapter.

E-commerce has quickly become an accepted means of conducting business. In fact, customers often prefer the convenience of doing business over the Internet, finding it an efficient time-saver. Consumers' comfort level with Internet commerce has opened up the global market faster than any other medium. We now have virtually unlimited options.

CUSTOMER SERVICE IS E-CUSTOMER CONTACTS

As you can imagine, conducting your E-commerce business effectively requires yet another skill set.

Understanding what E-consumers expect from an online business—legitimacy, trustworthiness, and credibility—and meeting those expectations is the first step to welcoming your online customers into your business. Being accessible, responding quickly to e-mail queries, and promptly fulfilling customer requests builds trust and establishes credibility.

Communication, primarily handled through e-mail, necessitates good writing skills and proper grammar usage. Special care must be taken to make sure that what you write is accurate. Learn to write clearly by formulating your thoughts and conveying the correct message. This may well be the most important component of E-commerce customer service.

When you conduct business over the Internet, you open your door to the world. Learning how to interact successfully with people from different cultures reflects positively on your professionalism and willingness to satisfy all your customers.

Before we go into E-commerce customer service, let's focus on Web sites. How your company's site is designed can make the difference between loyal customers and frustrated surfers.

In your role as a consumer, think about some Web sites you visited recently. What was your impression of those Web sites?

In regard to those you viewed positively, *what was it about the sites that you liked?*

In regard to those you did not view positively, *what was it about the sites that you didn't like?*

Now think about your own Web site. Work through a typical Internet transaction as your customers would, from start to finish. Ask yourself the following questions:

■ *How easy was it for me to navigate through our site?*

■ *How quickly was I able to move from one page to another?*

■ *Was the ordering process easy and quick?*

■ *Would I do business online with my company?*

Focus on all aspects of the Web site, because your customers are going to. As a group, discuss ways in which you can make your Web site more visually appealing and easy to navigate. Find ways to build a winning Web site:

■ Keep text to a minimum. In general, people prefer a lot of white space when reading computer screens.

■ When using photos or other graphics, make sure they do not grind the surfing pace to a halt.

■ Make sure the ordering process is easy by monitoring the product information page, shopping cart, customer registration, billing information, and final checkout.

■ Include warranty or guarantee information and information about technical support, if appropriate, on your site.

■ Include a "contact the company" button for easy e-mailing.

■ Customers may learn about your company through a search engine, so select words and phrases for your title pages that they are likely to use for key word searches.

PICTURE THIS...

THE WRONG WAY TO HANDLE E-CUSTOMER CONTACTS

Mr. Bowman was interested in buying a new set of golf clubs and surfed the Internet for information. He used a key word search, and one of the Web sites he found offered the set he wanted at a good price. He was unclear about shipping charges and sent an e-mail query. Tom, an employee at the sporting goods store, replied to Mr. Bowman's e-mail as follows:

> The shipping charges to send the set of golf clubs you inquired about will be $3.00.
>
> Nineteenth Hole Golf Company

Tom hit the send button. Later he reviewed the e-mail and read— $3.00. He meant to type $30.00. Small mistake. Costly difference. How will Mr. Bowman feel if he had already placed his order and then finds out he was quoted the wrong shipping charges?

What Went Wrong?

Tom was hasty in hitting the send button without proofreading the e-mail. If the customer had already placed his order, Tom and his company would have had two options: either eat the cost of shipping or e-mail the customer with the correct quote. Neither of these options is ideal. For a small company, eating the difference in the cost of shipping can quickly cut into its profit margin.

How Did the Customer Feel?

Informing a customer you quoted an incorrect rate may cause him or her to lose faith in your company. It can even cost your company a sale and a potential future customer relationship. However Nineteenth Hole Company decides to handle this blunder, Mr. Bowman might form the opinion that it is not a credible company.

Valuing your E-prospects and giving them exceptional service online can turn prospective buyers into loyal customers. Customers who interact with a business over the Internet deserve the same level of service as face-to-face and telephone customers. Master the following steps and you will be able to handle any E-customer in any E-situation.

Step 1: What Does the E-Customer Expect?

Step 2: Hanging the Open Sign: Being Accessible

Step 3: Writing What You Mean: E-Mail Communication

Step 4: Speaking Around the World: Cross-Cultural Etiquette

In the contact between Tom and Mr. Bowman, if Tom had carefully read the e-mail before hitting the send button, he would have caught and corrected the mistake. Now he is caught in a dilemma.

STEP 1
WHAT DOES THE E-CUSTOMER EXPECT?

When you do business over the Internet, you open your door to customers around the globe. Your e-customers can be anybody from anywhere. Consider this: Customers who transact business over the Internet put their blind faith in your company. Always strive to give them the same level of customer service you give your local customers.

When potential customers enter your E-business, they have no idea what your brick-and-mortar business looks like. They cannot tell if your company is a multimillion-dollar corporation, a small business run out of a strip mall location, or a one-person operation based from home. It does not matter how large or small your company is; what does matter is that you handle all your e-customers with professionalism and courtesy.

E-Customers Want to Know You Are Legitimate

Your home page is your customer's first step into your door. How your "door step" is laid out can either invite customers in or cause them to navigate elsewhere. On your home page, let your visitors know that you are a legitimate company, that you stand behind your products, and explain your service and product guarantees. Your customers want to know that you care enough about them to guarantee their satisfaction. Reiterating this in all e-mail correspondence will make a positive impression.

E-Customers Want to Know You Are Trustworthy

You show you are trustworthy by the manner in which you interact with your customers. Promptly answering e-mail queries is a great way to begin building a trusting relationship. When customers place online orders, they want to know their order was processed. When you demonstrate to customers you are reliable and informative by responding quickly and thoroughly through E-communication, they will feel more comfortable placing their trust in you and your company.

E-Customers Want to Know You Will Do What You Say You Will When You Say You Will

Handle your e-customers as expeditiously as if they came into your business or called you on the phone. When customers ask questions, they want prompt replies. When they place orders, they want a speedy turnaround. Think about this: If a customer sends you an e-mail query and you take a week to answer it or answer it in a haphazard manner, you are going to lose credibility. Your potential customers may wonder, if it takes so long to respond to an e-mail, how long will it take to process an order or handle a problem? Responding to e-mail queries promptly shows you care about your e-customers.

E-Customers Want to Establish a Relationship with You

When customers e-mail you for information, they like to know they are dealing with a human being. Always put a human touch and reflect your personality in your replies. Picture yourself as communicating with a customer who is in your business. Let your personality come through in your e-mails by being responsive, friendly, and professional at all times.

PICTURE THIS...
A BETTER WAY TO HANDLE E-CUSTOMERS

Tom's initial reply to Mr. Bowman looked like a stock text that he copied into an e-mail. A better response would have been:

> The shipping charges to send the complete set will be $30.00. We stand behind all our equipment. Your satisfaction is always guaranteed.
>
> We look forward to hearing from you and doing business with you.
>
> Sincerely,
> Nineteenth Hole Golf Company

How Did the Customer Feel?

This e-mail was an improvement over the first. Tom added a human touch by showing his interest in doing business with Mr. Bowman. Mr. Bowman appreciated that this company included a "satisfaction guaranteed" phrase in the e-mail, because it indicated that the company stood behind its product.

STEP 2
HANGING THE OPEN SIGN:
BEING ACCESSIBLE

When you conduct business over the Internet, customers feel welcome twenty-four hours a day, seven days a week. It is important to be accessible since your e-customers have no idea whether you are a one-person operation or a business that employs thousands.

TIP

If you are not able to be accessible 24/7, let your customers know when you are open. If you are closed weekends, specify this on your Web site so that customers who e-mail you Friday evening will not look for a reply throughout the weekend. Also, be sure to note all contact information on your site, including your physical address (or post office box number) and phone and fax numbers, if appropriate.

Respond to All E-Queries Promptly

You build credibility as a company by being responsive to existing and potential customers. Give your e-customers the same consideration you would if they were face-to-face with you. Thank customers for their interest in your company and products. Anticipate other questions they may have and address them in your e-mails. In other words, always give more than is asked for.

Process Requests Quickly

When customers do business over the Internet they want to know their requests and orders will be handled right away. When an order has been shipped, send an e-mail confirmation. Thank the customer for the order, summarize what was shipped, when it was shipped, and provide tracking information. When an item is backordered, let the customer know the approximate shipping date. Assure them that you will not bill his or her credit card until the item is shipped, and provide an option to cancel a delayed order.

Build Customer Loyalty Through E-Mailing

Always thank customers for their interest in your company. Use e-mails to tell customers about sales, discounts, or new products. Send information to your repeat customers to let them know about special events and updates about your company. Always include an opt-out for those customers who do not want to receive unsolicited e-mails. If you deal with the same e-customers repeatedly, keep in contact by sending *thinking of you* or *how are you doing e-mails*. Keeping your company's name in the customers' minds can generate additional sales, and it tells them you value their business.

PICTURE THIS...
A BETTER WAY TO RESPOND TO E-MAIL QUERIES

In this e-mail reply, Tom included additional information he felt Mr. Bowman would need before placing his order:

> Thank you for your interest in the Magnum-18 Golf Clubs. The shipping charges to send the complete set will be $30.00. All in-stock items are shipped by the following business day. We are closed weekends, so any orders placed on Friday will be shipped the following Monday.
>
> We stand behind all our equipment. Your satisfaction is always guaranteed.
>
> We look forward to hearing from you. If you would like to be informed about special sales, please respond to this e-mail, and I will be happy to add you to our e-mail list.
>
> Sincerely,
> Nineteenth Hole Golf Company

How Did the Customer Feel?

Mr. Bowman felt good about the company after reading this e-mail. He liked the fact that Tom answered his questions about ordering and shipping before he asked.

STEP 3
WRITING WHAT YOU MEAN: E-MAIL COMMUNICATION

Tom's third e-mail is much better than his first. As you saw, it is easy to make a mistake. When keyboarding is your means of communication, chances for miscommunication increase.

Use Good Writing Skills

On the subject line, write a short phrase that reflects the content of your e-mail. For example, Order Confirmation tells your customer exactly what the e-mail pertains to. In the body of the letter, interject phrases like *yes, I'll be happy to take care of that*, *absolutely*, or *I've taken care of that for you*. Using the same words in e-mails that you use in verbal communication interjects your personality into your e-conversations. Writing *Thank you for doing business. . . .* or *We appreciate your business. . . .* reflects positively on your company as well.

Begin with a Salutation

Beginning your e-mails with a personal greeting, such as *Dear Mr. Bowman. . . .* is a nice touch that customers will appreciate. If you do not know the name, begin with a generic salutation reflective of your business. such as *Greetings from Nineteenth Hole Golf Company* or *Dear Fellow Golfer*.

Make Messages Visually Interesting

Keep your messages short and to the point. When customers see a long block of print, chances are they are going to skip over parts of the message. Use short sentences and action verbs to express yourself: *We shipped your order. . . .* rather than *The order was shipped.* Create white space in the body of your messages by using short paragraphs and double spacing. Using bullets or headings also creates interest.

Write as You Would Say It

If you are unsure of your wording, read the message out loud to hear how it sounds. Write clearly and specifically and put the most important items first. Your computer's spell-check tool will only spot misspellings, not improper grammar usage, so carefully proofread all messages word for word. Keep the shortcut lingo (such as lol, jk, btw, etc.) for your personal e-mails only. Never hit the send button until you have reread your message.

Add an Interesting Closing

This is a good place to display your company's personality by adding a line that shows you value your customer's business. Always sign with your name and title, rather than only your title or the name of your business.

PICTURE THIS...
THE RIGHT WAY TO RESPOND TO E-MAIL QUERIES

This time, Tom sent a great e-mail reply. He provided detailed information, validated that it was a great choice, and his enthusiasm and willingness to help came through to Mr. Bowman.

Dear Mr. Bowman,

Thank you for your interest in the Magnum-18 Golf Clubs. This is our most popular set of clubs. The shipping charges to send the complete set will be $30.00. I will be happy to take your order and answer any additional questions you may have.

- We ship all in-stock items by the following business day.
- We are closed weekends so any orders placed on Friday will be shipped the following Monday.
- We stand behind all our equipment. Your satisfaction is always guaranteed.

We look forward to hearing from you. If you would like to be informed about special sales, please respond to this e-mail; in the subject line type "add to list."

At Nineteenth Hole Golf Company we appreciate your business. Our customers always start on the first hole.

Sincerely,

Tom Campbell

Golf Sales Consultant

How Did the Customer Feel?

In this e-mail, Tom began by addressing Mr. Bowman by name. He answered Mr. Bowman's question first, interjected his personality by saying that this was a great choice, and said he would be happy to help with future needs. He used easy-to-understand words, kept paragraphs short, and used bullets to highlight company policies. Throughout the message, Tom used good communication skills. He included a phrase that reflects his company's attitude toward its customers. He ended with a good closing that included his name and title.

Mr. Bowman was impressed by Tom's quick response and detailed e-mail. He felt this company was credible, and he had developed enough trust in Nineteenth Hole to place his order. After it was shipped, Tom sent a confirming e-mail.

Mr. Bowman,

We shipped your order today for the following item:

* Magnum-18 Golf Club Complete Set

Our customers give us great feedback on these clubs, and I'm sure you'll enjoy using them. If you have any questions, please feel free to e-mail or call me. I will be glad to help you with any future needs.

Thank you for your order. At Nineteenth Hole Golf Company, we appreciate your business.

Sincerely,

Tom Campbell

Golf Sales Consultant

STEP 4
SPEAKING AROUND THE WORLD: CROSS-CULTURAL ETIQUETTE

The Internet has shrunk our world to the degree that it is smart business to learn how to communicate around the globe. We live in a world composed of many cultures, customs, and languages. Even though we may appear different, many communication skills are universal. Basic courtesies, respect, willingness to help, compassion, and a positive attitude are successful ways to communicate worldwide, even without understanding other languages.

Treat Other People as You Want to Be Treated

Did you know there is a version of the Golden Rule in every culture? The words, depending on the origin, are different from those you may have learned, but the meaning is the same. When you treat others with respect, consideration, courtesy, compassion, and kindness, you will be able to effectively work through any language or cultural barriers.

Read E-Mail Queries Carefully So You Will Be Able to "Listen" Well

People may write in a way that makes it difficult for you to understand the message when you first read it. When you receive an e-mail that is not clear, reread it carefully word for word to make sure you correctly understand the meaning.

Use Proper Grammar

Your e-customers may not understand jargon or slang. When you get in the habit of using correct grammar every time you speak and write, customers will find it easier to understand your message. Do not try to mimic other peoples' accents or manner of speaking. Be yourself and speak and write in your normal voice, yet be mindful that language differences may hamper communication effectiveness.

Be Professional

You show you are a professional by not stereotyping other people, by not talking down to others, and by not making assumptions. When you treat other people with dignity, you show respect and tolerance. Always be professional in your responses and give a complete explanation of any words or terms your e-customer might not understand.

The right combination to satisfying your Internet customers is to show that you are legitimate and trustworthy by being accessible and responding quickly and by doing everything you can to communicate clearly with all your online customers.

Give Your E-Customers the Same Quality of Service
You Give Your Face-to-Face and Telephone Customers

Using the Internet as a means of conducting business has its ups and downs.

The upside is that it can positively influence your bottom line. Opening your door globally can bring you unlimited sales and service opportunities that you do not have within your local community. You stand to gain a lot from a small investment.

The downside is that e-customers do not have the opportunity to get to know you like your local customers do. They may never develop a loyal relationship with you and your business.

You can turn that down into an up and improve your chances of developing a loyal e-customer base by giving your Internet customers the same level of service you give to your local customers.

A warm welcome on your home page, an easy to navigate site, a quick response to e-mail queries, and prompt order processing will increase your chance of online success. Quickly establishing trust and credibility and making it easy for your e-customers to do business with you can turn surfers into paying customers.

Welcoming any opportunity to build your business can improve your chances for success. When you provide each and every one of your customers with the best possible service, you take a huge step that may well see you through economic downturns.

- Demonstrate to your e-customers that you are trustworthy and credible.

- Go the extra mile for all your customers.

- Show that you appreciate all customers, especially those different from you.

- Remember that each of your customers is the reason you have a job.

KEY POINTS

Step 1: What Does the E-Customer Expect?

- E-customers want to know you are legitimate.
- E-customers want to know you are trustworthy.
- E-customers want to know you will do what you say you will when you say you will.
- E-customers want to establish a relationship with you.

Step 2: Hanging the Open Sign: Being Accessible

- Respond to e-queries promptly.
- Process requests quickly.
- Build customer loyalty through e-mailing.

Step 3: Writing What You Mean: E-Mail Communication

- Use good writing skills.
- Begin with a salutation.
- Make messages visually interesting.
- Write as you would say it.
- Add an interesting closing.

Step 4: Speaking Around the World: Cross-Cultural Etiquette

- Treat other people as you want to be treated.
- Read carefully so you will "listen" well.
- Use proper grammar.
- Be professional.

P R A C T I C E   L E S S O N

Step 1: What Does the E-Customer Expect?

Write down some things that are important to e-customers.

_____

_____

Step 2: Hanging the Open Sign: Being Accessible

What are some things your company can do on its Web site to show your e-customers that you are accessible?

_____

_____

Refer to the customer contact example you noted at the beginning of the chapter.

Step 3: Writing What You Mean: E-mail Communication

Write a typical e-mail request you might receive from a customer.

_____

_____

Now write a response to the customer.

_____

_____

Step 4: Speaking Around the World: Cross-Cultural Etiquette

What are some things you can do to better communicate with people from other countries?

_____

_____

D O I N G   I T   R I G H T

I'm a firm believer in supporting my local business community. It fosters good relations and, most of all, it boosts our local economy. I always strive to do business locally, yet there are numerous occasions when that is not possible.

In those instances, I admit I'm an online fanatic. I love everything about online shopping. I can do business when it's convenient for me. I can shop with my fingertips, surfing from site to site without getting stuck in traffic or calling a company that holds me up with a lengthy call answering system. And, with some companies, I can even chat online if necessary.

I'm also a Google fan. When I don't know where to shop or if I'm not sure exactly what I need, I can type any key word or phrase and in most instances have many options from which to choose.

It would be difficult for me to select one company to highlight because there are many great sites and online companies to which I have become loyal. When I find a site I don't care for, I surf until I find one I do care for.

The most important factors I look for when online shopping are credibility; trustworthiness; a visually appealing site; a quick response time to e-mail queries; an effortless ordering process; hassle-free returns; and a company that guarantees my satisfaction. When I find a site that meets the above criteria, I become a loyal online shopper.

Can your business benefit by conducting online business? If the answer is yes and you haven't yet created your site, then jump on the bandwagon. If you already have a site but aren't getting much online business, analyze what you can do to improve.

No matter how you conduct business, your number one goal should always be to make it easy for your customers to do business with you. That is your surefire way to find business success.

H O W   D O   I   M E A S U R E   U P ?

1. How well do I understand what my e-customers expect? What do
    I do to show that I am legitimate, trustworthy, and dependable?

    _____

    _____

    _____

2. How accessible are we to our online customers? When I receive
    e-mails do I respond quickly and process requests promptly?
    What can I do to improve?

    _____

    _____

    _____

3. How are my written communication skills? Are my e-mail messages
    visually interesting? Do I write as I speak? What areas need
    improvement?

    _____

    _____

    _____

4. When I interact with people of other cultures, what do I do
    differently to ensure I am communicating effectively? How can
    I improve?

    _____

    _____

    _____

CHAPTER

7

Giving When Getting Is Not Expected: Self-Service Contacts

A SURE WAY TO DELIGHT CUSTOMERS
IS TO FIND WAYS TO GIVE THEM
MORE THAN THEY EXPECT

Write down a typical customer contact that is reflective of your self-service interactions:

_____

_____

_____

_____

_____

Think about this scenario as you work through this chapter. Use it as the example when answering the Practice Lesson questions at the end of the chapter.

Customers today encounter self-service operations in dealing with many businesses. You can probably think of many situations in which you, as a customer, regularly make use of self-service, often with no interaction whatsoever with another human being. You can use self-checkout stations to pay for your purchases at most grocery, big box discount, and home improvement stores. You can withdraw money from your bank account on ATM machines available in stores and on the street. You can purchase gasoline at practically any service station with a swipe of your credit card. You can check in and check out of hotels using on-premise kiosks that many chains now offer their guests. And probably the most widely used self-service offerings you may often take advantage of are found on Web sites, where you can place an order, check its status, review your billing, and even pay your bills.

Self-service has made it easy for consumers to do business…when all goes well. The upsides of self-service are that it is convenient, quick, and efficient. It also offers you increased control over how you conduct your business. However, the operative words are "when all goes well." The downsides of self-service are that there is always a learning curve the first time you use a company's options, often no one is available to help when a problem is encountered, and the wait time can be longer than traditional interactions if the person ahead of you is confused or experiences a problem. An additional downside for some customers is that they do not want self-service options. They like the human touch and prefer interacting with a real person.

CUSTOMER SERVICE IS SELF-SERVICE CONTACTS

Offering basic courtesies, communicating well, and building relationships can be accomplished even when customers serve themselves. Most consumers have become comfortable with self-service and appreciate its convenience. However, self-service should never mean no service. Customers want to know an employee is available to help them, if needed. When you find ways to provide service in self-service settings, you will stand out in your customers' minds in a positive way.

Customers appreciate when an employee notices that assistance is needed and takes the time to offer help before it is requested. If you are in a business that offers self-checkout lines for your customers, greet the customers as they enter the self-checkout area, make eye contact, and let them know you are available if they need help. In-store settings offer a great opportunity to give customers more than they expect. When you are actively involved in observing and moving the flow along, you show that you are interested in your customers and appreciate their business.

If your business primarily handles phone contacts or is Web-based, provide clear instructions at the beginning of the contact as to how these customers can reach an employee.

Whether your self-service offerings are primarily in-store or phone- or Internet-based, you have a valuable opportunity to end all transactions on a positive note. Always thank your customers for choosing to do business with you. Leaving a positive lasting impression stays with them long after they finish their transactions. When you offer self-service options, your customers will appreciate the convenience—as long as you make the interaction convenient for them.

BRAINSTORM

Think about a recent self-service interaction in which you were the customer. What was your reaction to your contact with the business after serving yourself?

- *What did the business do that made you feel comfortable?*

- *Was help readily available when needed?*

- *When you completed your transaction, did the employee (or message on the automated phone system or Web site screen) say something that made you feel valued?*

Now, think about your business. Walk through a self-service contact, viewing it as though you are experiencing it for the first time. Then answer the questions above from a customer's standpoint.

Remember to pay close attention to all details—your customers will. Find ways to improve your self-service interactions. Review this process frequently to make sure that you always give your customers, both self-service and traditional, more than they expect.

PICTURE THIS...
THE WRONG WAY TO HANDLE SELF-SERVICE INTERACTIONS

Tina stopped by the grocery store to pick up the items she needed to make dinner. This was part of her usual routine on her way home from work, and she usually did it with little thought: she'd run in, grab a basket, find the items on her list, and then find the shortest checkout line.

Today was different, though. For some reason, every checkout counter had at least two people waiting in line. She looked over to the self-checkout area and noticed one of the cash registers was available. She had never attempted self-checkout before but decided to give it a try after noticing a cashier standing at a podium in that area.

Tina set her basket down on the shelf and read the screen. After a few tries, she successfully scanned the bar code on her first item and placed it in the bag. She then found the bar code on her second item and scanned it as well. But this time, when she placed it in the bag, she heard a recorded voice saying, "Place the item in the bag." *It is in the bag*, she thought. The voice sounded again. "Place the item in the bag." Embarrassed, she lifted the item and put it back in the bag, which stopped the voice.

Noticing another customer waiting to use the self-checkout, Tina hurriedly picked up the next item in her basket, which was a bunch of broccoli. There was no bar code to scan. She read the screen and touched the button for produce. The screen prompted her to enter the four-digit number. *What four-digit number?* When Tina could not find a four-digit number on the broccoli, she looked to the podium where the employee had been standing, but no one was there.

Now she noticed that two customers were waiting. Tina felt so frustrated and embarrassed by not knowing what to do that she gathered up her items and left the self-checkout area. When she saw the regular checkout lines were still long, she made a quick decision. *I think we'll order takeout tonight.* She quickly put her items back and left the grocery store without making a purchase.

What Went Wrong?

Let's begin by noting what went right. Tina made the decision to try the self-checkout lanes because she noticed an employee appeared to be available for assistance if she ran into any trouble. Had that employee been paying attention when Tina began checking out, he would have seen that she was inexperienced. This would have been a great training moment for the employee to show Tina how to use the screen and scanner, but because Tina became frustrated when she needed assistance and no one was available, the experience left a negative impression. As a result, she would not likely use the self-checkout lane again any time soon.

How Did the Customer Feel?

Even though Tina felt uncomfortable, she was willing to try self-checkout. She was embarrassed when the voice told her to put her items in the bag and when she could not find the appropriate product codes to enter. Then, when she noticed someone was waiting behind her, she felt even more embarrassed because she was moving slowly. Finally, she became so frustrated that she walked away in the middle of her transaction and opted to buy no groceries at all.

When you offer self-service to your customers, you offer them increased convenience and control over the way they do business with you. The most important thing is that you find ways to provide great service in self-service situations. Always look for ways to help your customers, even those who are comfortable helping themselves.

Learn the following and you will provide exceptional service to your self-service customers:

Step 1: Saying Hello: Greeting the Customer

Step 2: Between Hello and Goodbye: Looking for Opportunities to Help

Step 3: Saying Goodbye: Ending the Transaction

Tina's poor first impression of self-checkout was her last impression of self-checkout. Had the employee taken the time to ease her discomfort by showing her how to use the screen and scanner, Tina would have gained confidence to try it again in the future.

STEP 1
SAYING HELLO: GREETING THE CUSTOMER

Even when customers are willing to serve themselves, they like to know an employee is nearby. Greeting your customers with a welcoming statement will put any customer at ease, even those using a self-service option for the first time.

An Employee Should Always Be Available

This is the most important goal of accustoming customers to using your self-service option. There is always a learning curve associated with moving into a new practice. Just as you need time to teach or learn new company procedures, policies, and products, your customers need time to learn and feel comfortable using self-service.

Say Hello to Every Customer

Greet every customer who chooses to use your self-service options. In in-store settings, smile, make eye contact, say hello, and give the customer your name. If your company uses automated phone answering, include in your greeting an option to reach a live person by offering an extension-number or dial-zero option. For Web site interactions, clearly state on your home page how a customer may reach a person. This can be done by providing an 800 number, a contact form, or a live-chat option. Offering a warm greeting to your self-service customers will help you begin to make a great first impression with them.

Tell the Customer You Are Available to Help

After your greeting, tell the customer you are available if they need help. Always make sure someone is available and be on the lookout for customers who need assistance.

PICTURE THIS...
THE RIGHT WAY TO GREET SELF-SERVICE CUSTOMERS

Tina stopped by the grocery store to pick up the items she needed to make dinner. This was part of her usual routine on her way home from work, and she usually did it with little thought: she'd run in, grab a basket, find the items on her list, and then find the shortest checkout line.

Today was different, though. For some reason, every checkout line had at least two people waiting. She noticed that one of the cash registers in the self-checkout area was available. She had never attempted self-checkout before, but decided to give it a try, particularly after noticing a cashier standing at a podium in the self-check area.

Tina set her basket down on the shelf and, before she looked at the screen, the cashier at the podium said, "Hello, my name is Ted. I'll be right here if you need any help."

"Thank you," Tina replied. She turned back to the screen and began reading it.

How Did the Customer Feel?
Tina was still uncomfortable, but when Ted smiled, made eye contact, and greeted her warmly, she felt less discomfort knowing help was available. She began forming a positive first impression.

STEP 2
BETWEEN HELLO AND GOODBYE: LOOKING FOR OPPORTUNITIES TO HELP

For the most part, customers who choose self-service are not going to need help. They will move through the process with ease, even when using the self-service option for the first time. However, problems are going to occur, and a problem can affect even the most experienced user. In in-store situations, a computer might glitch. In phone situations, the automated system may not be the best option for every contact. Customers may have a question not covered by the options offered, or they may need to discuss something with an employee. By staying aware and looking for opportunities where you can help, you let your customers know they are your first priority.

Monitor the Flow

This is easiest to do in in-store settings because you can spot customers who are inexperienced or look confused. By observing the flow of self-service cash registers and kiosks, you will be in a position to step in and help when needed. By watching for lines that are backed up, you will be able to find out why bottlenecks are occurring and do what is necessary to move the process along. In phone and Web interactions, of course, you cannot know when your customers need help. In these situations, offering a way to reach an employee is the best option you can provide to increase your customers' comfort level with self-service.

Look for Teaching Moments

Again, this is easiest when you are face-to-face with your customers. Be on the lookout for ways to teach customers how to best use your self-service equipment. Step in before customers become so frustrated that, like Tina, they leave the area and perhaps even your place of business. The path of least resistance will be for you to take over for your customers.

However, when you do this, your customers are not learning, and they may encounter the same problem in the future. Rather, offer to train them. Show your customers what to do, but allow them to work through the complete transaction by moving through screens and entering their own information.

For phone and Web interactions, your teaching moments are likely to come after a customer tells you about a problem. Take the time to walk each customer through the transaction. If you encounter the same complaint repeatedly, let your manager know so that it can be remedied.

Make Your Self-Service Customers Feel Valued

Whether you provide service in traditional settings or through self-service, you can find ways to make your customers feel valued. In self-service situations, the best way to do this is by communicating to your customers that you are happy to help and then looking for ways to do so. When customers feel valued, you are building a positive relationship, and they will be more likely to use your business's self-service options again.

TIP

If you work in a retail store and are assigned to the self-service checkout area, try getting out from behind your podium. From time to time, walk around or stand in the center of the area. Customers will see you as approachable and willing to help.

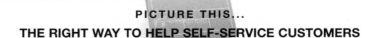

PICTURE THIS...
THE RIGHT WAY TO HELP SELF-SERVICE CUSTOMERS

Ted noticed that Tina was inexperienced and he thought that this was most likely her first time using the self-checkout counter. When she tried, unsuccessfully, to scan her first item, he paid close attention so he would know if she needed help.

Finally, after a few tries, she successfully scanned her first item and placed it in the bag. She found the bar code on her second item and scanned it. When she placed it in the bag, she heard a recorded voice, "Place the item in the bag."

"I don't know why that happens," Ted said as he walked over to Tina. "Sometimes the weight isn't picked up. Try picking up the can and putting it back in the bag."

Tina did as Ted suggested, and the voice stopped. Feeling a little embarrassed, she smiled at Ted. He noticed someone was waiting to check out, so he backed up but stayed in the center of the checkout area.

When Tina placed her broccoli on the scanner and looked confused, Ted walked back over to her. "The screen is going to prompt you to enter a four-digit number. If you can't find it on the produce, the items are listed on this roller." Ted pointed above the screen and showed Tina how to find broccoli.

"Thank you so much for helping me. I wouldn't have a clue where to find the code." Tina scanned the rest of her items. Ted stood by and then walked her through the pay process.

How Did the Customer Feel?

Because Ted stepped in to help, Tina felt comfortable learning the self-checkout process. She appreciated that he came to her assistance before she asked for it. She also appreciated that he took the time to train her.

STEP 3
SAYING GOODBYE:
ENDING THE INTERACTION

When you take the time to properly end self-service contacts, you go a long way toward making your customers feel that they are valued and that they matter to you.

Make Sure Customers Are Satisfied

Asking a simple question such as, "Did you find everything you needed?" or "Is there anything else we can do for you?" or "How is everything?" will help you know if your customer is satisfied. Of course, the best way to determine satisfaction is by observing your self-service customers during transactions. You will know by their facial expressions and body language whether they are comfortable or uncomfortable, at ease or frustrated. When you pay attention to your customers, you should have a good idea of their satisfaction level. If, through body language, you think someone is not satisfied, ask "How can I help you?" Don't let a self-service customer leave without making sure you did all you could to help make their experience a positive one.

Thank Customers for Their Business

Always, thank your customers for doing business with you. In person, say "Thank you for _____. Fill in the blank as appropriate: coming into our store"; doing business with us"; being our customer." On the phone, include a thank you message before ending an automated contact. On Web sites, post a thank you or we appreciate your business message on the final screen.

PICTURE THIS...
THE RIGHT WAY TO END SELF-SERVICE CONTACTS

After Tina paid and gathered her bags, Ted asked, "Did everything else go okay for you?"

"Yes, thanks for all your help. I couldn't have done it without you," Tina said with a laugh.

"Anything can be a little frustrating the first time you try. Thanks for sticking with it, and thanks for coming in tonight."

"Thank you for helping me. Bye." Tina walked out of the store completely satisfied with her experience. Her first impression of using the self-checkout was a positive one.

How Did the Customer Feel?

Tina felt valued when Ted asked if everything went okay. By easing her discomfort and providing great service in a no-service situation, Tina felt the store employees truly cared about their customers. She had always liked shopping at this store for its convenience; now she felt even more loyal about giving it her business.

PICTURE THIS...
PUTTING IT ALL TOGETHER

Tina stopped by the grocery store to pick up the items she needed to make dinner. This was part of her usual routine on her way home from work, and she usually did it with little thought: she'd run in, grab a basket, find the items on her list, and then find the shortest checkout line.

Today was different, though. For some reason, every checkout line had at least two people waiting. She noticed that one of the cash registers in the self-checkout area was available. She had never attempted self-checkout before, but decided to give it a try, particularly after noticing a cashier standing at a podium in the self-check area.

Tina set her basket down on the shelf and before she looked at the screen, the cashier at the podium said, "Hello, my name is Ted. I'll be right here if you need any help."

"Thank you," Tina replied. She turned back to the screen and began reading it.

Ted noticed that Tina was inexperienced, and he thought that this was most likely her first time using the self-checkout counter. When she tried, unsuccessfully, to scan her first item, he paid close attention so he would know if she needed help.

Finally, after a few tries she successfully scanned her first item and placed it in the bag. She found the bar code on her second item and scanned it. When she placed it in the bag, she heard a recorded voice, "Place the item in the bag."

"I don't know why that happens," Ted said as he walked over to Tina. "Sometimes the weight isn't picked up. Try picking up the can and putting it back in the bag."

Tina did as Ted suggested and the voice stopped. Feeling a little embarrassed, she smiled at Ted. He noticed someone was waiting to check out, so he backed up but stayed in the center of the checkout area.

When Tina placed her broccoli on the scanner and looked confused, Ted walked back over to her. "The screen is going to prompt you to enter a four-digit number. If you can't find it on the produce, the items are listed on this roller." Ted pointed above the screen and showed Tina how to find broccoli.

"Thank you so much for helping me. I wouldn't have a clue where to find the code." Tina scanned the rest of her items. Ted stood by and then walked her through the pay process.

After Tina paid and gathered her bags, Ted asked, "Did everything else go okay for you?"

"Yes, thanks for all your help. I couldn't have done it without you," Tina said with a laugh.

"Anything can be a little frustrating the first time you try. Thanks for sticking with it, and thanks for coming in tonight."

"Thank you for helping me. Bye." Tina walked out of the store completely satisfied with her experience. Her first impression of using the self-checkout was a positive one.

Whether you provide service through traditional channels or by offering self-service options to your customers, you can always find ways to incorporate basic courtesies, communicate well, and build relationships. You can always give your customers more than they expect. Customers are not going to set high expectations when they serve themselves; when you give them the same consideration you do your traditional customers, you show how much you value each and every one of your customers.

A Sure Way to Delight Customers Is to Find
Ways to Give Them More Than They Expect

Many businesses are finding ways to integrate self-service options for their customers. Your business may be considering installing self-serve kiosks or checkout lanes. You may already have an automated phone answering system that provides options for customers without any human contact. Or you may provide a Web site for your customers to place orders, review account information, or to pay bills.

There are many great reasons to implement self-service. From a customer standpoint, you are providing a quick, efficient, and convenient way to conduct business. From a business perspective, it saves time, money, and resources, and it allows you to reassign employees to other functions.

Whichever way you view your implementation of self-service, make the transition go smoothly by training customers how to use the self-service equipment and then providing exceptional service. Taking these steps will ensure a long-lasting, positive experience for both customers and employees.

Before implementing self-service options, plan how you will train customers, as well as provide exceptional customer service. Write down specific procedures and goals. Doing a great job with all your customers will go far in seeing you through the transition period.

- Making customers happy is your first priority.

- Always stay tuned in to your customers.

- Find innovative ways to stand out—positively—in your customers' minds.

- Include in your goal plan ways to give your customers more than they expect.

K E Y   P O I N T S

Step 1: Saying Hello: Greeting the Customer

- An employee should always be available.
- Say hello to every customer.
- Tell the customer you are available to help.

Step 2: Between Hello and Goodbye: Looking for Opportunities to Help

- Monitor the flow.
- Look for teaching moments.
- Make your self-service customers feel valued.

Step 3: Saying Goodbye: Ending the Interaction

- Make sure customers are satisfied.
- Thank customers for their business.

P R A C T I C E   L E S S O N

Refer to the customer contact example you noted at the beginning of the chapter.

Step 1: Saying Hello: Greeting the Customer

How will you greet self-service customers?

What can you say and do to let customers know you are available to help?

_____

_____

Step 2: Between Hello and Goodbye: Looking for Opportunities to Help

What specific steps will you take to observe the self-service flow?

_____

_____

How will you approach customers and what will you say when you see a teaching opportunity?

_____

_____

What can you do to make your self-service customers know you value them?

_____

_____

Step 3: Saying Goodbye: Ending the Interaction

What can you do to make sure your self-service customers are satisfied?

_____

_____

What will you say to customers when they are finished?

_____

_____

D O I N G   I T   R I G H T !

I appreciate the convenience of self-service options. When all goes right, I can get the job done quickly and efficiently. I can get in and out of my grocery store quickly when I only need a few items. I can pump and pay for gas without waiting in line for a cashier. ATMs may be my favorite self-service option; I often wonder how I got by before I was able to get cash whenever I needed it. I order airline tickets online, and I appreciate being able to check in online the day before my flight. All in all, I think most consumers would agree that self-service has made life easier for us, which is a good thing in our speed-of-light-paced world.

When choosing an online company, if I can't verify the legitimacy of a small company I often turn to one of the large marketplace sites. These companies have proven track records, and they offer me so many choices that my ordering opportunities seem endless. The ones I do business with give me help options to contact them, and they resolve problems quickly and to my satisfaction.

No matter what site I choose to do business with, I do so because I have established a comfort level with the company. What is most important to me in any online transaction with any size company is knowing a person is available to help. I want to know that if I have a question or run into a problem I can call them or send an e-mail. I want the assurance that any problems will be handled correctly and promptly and that my satisfaction is guaranteed.

Large marketplace sellers may have more resources and dollars to spend on self-service options than your company does, but small companies should not be deterred. The single most important thing you can do, in providing self-service, is to ensure that the process is easy, that you offer help options, that you respond quickly to resolve problems, and that you provide exceptional customer service.

Remember, self-service never means no service. Self-service means finding ways to serve your customers when they aren't expecting service. When you successfully do that, they will be more likely to put your company on their favorites list.

H O W   D O   I   M E A S U R E   U P ?

1. When I handle self-service, do I greet every customer and let them know I am available to help? What can I do to make sure I remember this step?

    _____

    _____

    _____

    _____

2. How effective and efficient am I in monitoring the flow of self-service customers? When I notice a teaching opportunity, do I handle it in a way that shows customers I value them? If not, how can I teach myself to do better?

    _____

    _____

    _____

    _____

3. Do I make sure all my customers are satisfied with their self-service experience? Do I remember to thank them for doing business with us? What do I need to do to improve in this area?

    _____

    _____

    _____

    _____

CHAPTER

8

Calming the Storm:
Difficult Customer Contacts

**WHEN A CUSTOMER COMPLAINS,
LOOK AT IT AS AN OPPORTUNITY TO IMPROVE**

Write down a customer contact you handled in which a customer was dissatisfied with your company:

_____

_____

_____

_____

_____

Think about the scenario above as you work through this chapter. Use it as the example when answering the Practice Lesson questions at the end of the chapter.

You have covered a lot of ground so far. You learned how to effectively communicate and build relationships with your customers. You learned special skills to interact with customers face to face, by telephone, and online. You developed valuable techniques to effectively handle your customers, but what about the customer who is difficult to deal with? A difficult customer can rattle even the most competent, the most confident customer service employee. Learning how to deal with a difficult customer will give you the self-assurance to effectively help each and every one of your customers in any situation.

CUSTOMER SERVICE IS DIFFICULT CUSTOMER CONTACTS

Customers may be difficult to deal with for several reasons. They may be upset because something was mishandled by your company, frustrated about a delay in handling a request, impatient about your company's response time, or maybe they are just having a bad day and taking their frustration out on you. Whatever a customer's reason for being difficult, how well you handle each situation can determine whether they remain your customer.

Handling difficult customer contacts requires special skills. Assuring the customer you can help and then listening carefully will enable you to determine the reason why the customer is being difficult. When you investigate what went wrong, you will identify the root cause of the problem. This will lead you to the best solution. Thanking the customer for allowing you to make things right enables you to restore your relationship, and following up to make sure the customer is satisfied makes you stand out as someone who truly cares about customer service. Taking the extra step to analyze what went wrong helps to fix any practices or procedures that need to be fixed.

PICTURE THIS...

THE WRONG WAY TO HANDLE DIFFICULT CUSTOMERS

Mike is a service representative for an appliance repair company. He has held this job for five years and is experienced in handling customers. However, Mike does not feel comfortable handling difficult customers and can easily become defensive. When he received a call from Mr. Roberts, here is what happened:

"ABC Appliance Repair, this is Mike speaking."

"Mike, this is Mr. Roberts. My service contract number is ACH2234. I'm not very happy right now. I called early this morning, and you were supposed to send a service person before noon. Now it's twelve thirty, and no one's showed."

"Hold on," Mike responded with a slight tinge of rudeness in his voice.

"Hold on? I don't want to hold on. My time is valuable, and I don't have all day to wait around. I want to know how soon someone will be out."

"Mr. Roberts, you need to hold while I check on this for you. We don't make a habit of making appointments we can't keep. We don't normally tell people we'll be out if we don't have someone to send out."

"I'm telling you someone was supposed to be here."

"I'm checking our records. . . . OK, I see what happened. Looks like when you called this morning we did tell you we could send a person right out, but you said you were going to call back to schedule the service call. We have no record that you called us back. I can schedule you for service tomorrow."

"I'm not waiting until tomorrow. I told the employee I would call back if I couldn't rearrange my schedule. She told me I was scheduled for this morning. The appointment was set. Tomorrow isn't satisfactory. I want someone out now."

"Evidently you told the rep you were going to call back. That's what she noted on the record. If you had scheduled an appointment when you spoke to her we would have sent someone out."

"I know what was said in our conversation, and I know I was scheduled for service this morning."

"Well, the soonest we can be out is tomorrow."

"Tomorrow isn't satisfactory. I've been sitting home all morning waiting for the service person."

"We don't have service people just sitting here waiting for calls. Everyone has already been dispatched today."

"Obviously I'm not getting through to you. I had an appointment for this morning. The person hasn't arrived. I need a person out this afternoon. Let me speak to a supervisor."

What Went Wrong?

In this contact, just about everything went wrong. When Mike received this call, it was clear that there had been a miscommunication. This was a case of he said/she said. Mike became defensive, sided with the employee, and spoke to the customer in a rude tone. When he blamed the customer for the miscommunication, Mr. Roberts asked for a supervisor.

How Did the Customer Feel?

Mr. Roberts became more upset as the conversation progressed. The manner in which Mike spoke to him and then blamed him for causing the miscommunication caused Mr. Roberts to feel he needed a supervisor to handle his problem.

It is not always easy to know what to say or how to handle customers who are upset from the moment you begin your conversation. However, satisfying a customer who is angry, upset, aggressive, or even rude can be accomplished in any situation. How well you are able to calm difficult customers will make the difference between satisfying them and furthering their feelings of frustration.

Most customers have legitimate reasons for complaining. By listening carefully and putting yourself in each customer's shoes, you will understand why he or she is being difficult. Occasionally, you will deal with customers who have no basis for their complaints. By learning how to tactfully handle a difficult customer in these situations, you will develop the skills to make every customer feel you did your best.

Master and practice the five-step process below, and you will have the ammunition you need to handle any customer in any situation.

Step 1: What Is Going on: Determine the Reason for the Problem

Step 2: What Caused the Problem: Identify the Root Cause

Step 3: What Can I Do: Rectify the Situation

Step 4: What Can I Say: Restore the Relationship

Step 5: What Needs to Be Done: Fix What Needs to Be Fixed

In the contact with Mr. Roberts, Mike could have done many things differently. He should have apologized and listened to Mr. Roberts. Who was right and who was wrong was not important. Mike should have focused on solving the problem, rather than on assigning blame. His rude tone and defensive attitude were not what Mr. Roberts wanted to hear. Mr. Roberts' perception was that he had an appointment. And while who was right and who was wrong was not important, Mr. Roberts' perception of the situation was important. Who is to blame should never matter when dealing with a customer who is angry or upset. Making the transition from a difficult customer to a satisfied customer should always be your number one goal.

STEP 1
WHAT IS GOING ON: DETERMINE THE REASON FOR THE PROBLEM

The first step is the most critical. What you say and how you say it are important. Your customer is upset, and you do not want to do anything to make him or her more frustrated.

Apologize

The first words out of your mouth should be, "I'm sorry." It is the right thing to do whether or not your company is at fault. Whenever someone or something causes customers to be upset, apologizing will let them know you care. Assure the customer you are going to help. In your opening statement, tell them you will do what you can to resolve the problem. When you give your assurance up front, it can help put your customer in a different frame of mind.

Restate the Customer's Opening Statement

Customers who are upset or angry may not communicate well. They may ramble, raise their voices, and be unable to clearly communicate their problem. By first restating their opening statement, you will make sure you are on the right track.

Listen Carefully

After assuring the customer you are going to help, listen to the details of the problem without interrupting. Listen to the complaint, and you will discover why the customer is being difficult. Mr. Roberts' complaint was that the service person was supposed to be dispatched in the morning. He was being difficult because he felt frustrated. He had spent valuable time waiting for the service person, and no one came. By actively listening to what the customer is saying rather than the way it is being said, you will be able to focus on solving the problem. If the customer is having trouble articulating the complaint, say something like, "Please tell me what happened when you called earlier."

Write Down Key Details

Pay attention to clues that will help you understand what happened. Make note of details that will help you solve the problem, such as the date or time the customer had called previously, what he or she was told by whom, and what actually happened.

Display Empathy

Before you proceed, let the customer know that you understand his or her feelings. Reassure again that you will help. Try to put yourself in your customer's shoes. No matter how a customer speaks to you, look at the problem from his or her perspective. You will be surprised how much clearer the problem will be when you see the situation from the customer's vantage point rather than your own.

Remain Composed

It is important that you stay composed from the beginning of your contact with a difficult customer. A customer speaking angrily or condescendingly may cause you to react in the same manner and tone. Becoming defensive and mirroring a customer's behavior will only agitate the customer further. By maintaining self-control, you will give yourself time to analyze the cause for the customer's anger. When you remain calm, the customer will begin to calm down.

TIP

In most cases, a difficult customer is not angry at you personally. Even if the customer refers to the company as you, as Mr. Roberts did with Mike, and you know you personally were not the cause of the problem, remember that the customer sees you as the company. Focus solely on solving the problem to keep from becoming defensive.

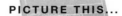

PICTURE THIS...

THE RIGHT WAY TO DETERMINE THE REASON FOR THE PROBLEM

"ABC Appliance Repair, this is Mike speaking."

"Mike, this is Mr. Roberts. My service contract number is ACH2234. I'm not very happy right now. I called early this morning, and you were supposed to send a service person before noon. Now it's twelve thirty, and no one's showed."

"Mr. Roberts, I am so sorry that happened. I'll be happy to help you. Now, you had a service appointment scheduled for this morning?"

"Yes, that's correct. I called first thing. The employee I spoke with told me she could send someone out this morning. I've been waiting all morning, and no one came. I'm a busy person, and my time is valuable. I need someone out right away."

"I understand. I'll need to check our records to see what happened. Can you hold while I do that?"

"Yes, I'll hold."

How Did the Customer Feel?

By apologizing and assuring Mr. Roberts that he would resolve the problem, Mike helped him calm down. Mr. Roberts appreciated that Mike listened carefully and displayed empathy when he said he understood his frustration. Mr. Roberts also appreciated Mike's confident and calm demeanor. He felt that Mike would work to resolve the problem.

TIP

If an angry customer immediately asks for your manager or the owner of your company without first giving you a chance to help, try this approach: "Ms. Customer, please give me the opportunity to resolve the problem. I'm confident that I will be able to help you, but if you are still not satisfied, I will personally refer your problem to my manager (or owner)." Your confident manner will give the customer the peace of mind that you are truly interested in resolving her problem.

If a customer uses profanity, calmly say "Mr. Customer, I understand you are upset, and I am going to help you, but there is no reason to use profanity." In most cases, the customer will stop. If it continues, calmly say, "I am going to work with you to resolve your problem. Will you please explain to me what happened without using profanity?" Again, by maintaining a calm demeanor, your customer will begin to calm down.

STEP 2
WHAT CAUSED THE PROBLEM: IDENTIFY THE ROOT CAUSE

Once you determine why the customer is upset, your next step is to figure out the cause of the problem. In Mr. Roberts' case, Mike should have a clear idea of the complaint. Mr. Roberts called earlier and scheduled a morning appointment. He was upset because it was past noon and no one had been out. Mike must now figure out what caused the problem.

Investigate the Situation

Mike asked Mr. Roberts to hold so he could find out what happened. This allowed Mike some time to review Mr. Roberts' account record and the store's appointment book. If the investigation will take longer than a reasonable hold time, make a specific commitment to get back to the customer.

TIP

When you need to review information before responding to a customer, think about the length of time you will need and offer a realistic time frame within which you will call back rather than promising to respond "as soon as possible" or "right away." Terms like these mean different things to different people. "Right away" might mean sometime today to you—it could mean within fifteen minutes to your customer. In addition, if your customer is dissatisfied with your commitment, try saying, "That's the best I can do in order to find out what happened."

Determine If the Customer Has a Valid Complaint

After investigating, determine whether the customer's complaint is legitimate. Most likely it will be. Even if you cannot determine a valid cause for the customer's complaint, it may still be prudent to rule in favor of the customer. In Mr. Roberts' situation, Mike did not know who was responsible for the miscommunication. He only knew that the misunderstanding had occurred between Mr. Roberts and the first employee. Mr. Roberts had expected a service person to be dispatched that morning. Mike should assume that Mr. Roberts' perception was correct.

Apologize Again If Necessary

If your investigation leads to the conclusion that someone within your company is at fault, take responsibility and apologize again. In any case, apologizing again reiterates your concern and desire to make things right with the difficult customer.

Explain What Happened

Keep the emotion out of your voice and stick to the facts. Be truthful, even when it means saying your company made a mistake. The customer may not like to hear what you are saying, but your honesty will be appreciated. Customers respect employees who are honest and upfront. Covering up, being evasive, or lying is never a good business policy.

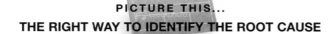

PICTURE THIS...
THE RIGHT WAY TO IDENTIFY THE ROOT CAUSE

"Yes, I'll hold."

"Mr. Roberts, thank you for holding. I checked our records, and again, I apologize that we weren't out this morning. When you spoke to the employee earlier, she was under the assumption that you needed to call back to schedule your appointment. We didn't hear back from you and therefore never scheduled the service call."

How Did the Customer Feel?

Mike took the time to investigate and determine the cause of the problem. Because he did not speak to Mr. Roberts on the first call, he had no way of knowing what was actually said. He could not determine whether the customer's complaint was valid because it was the result of a miscommunication. He apologized and stayed neutral when he explained what happened. By staying neutral, Mike did not take or assign blame and that helped Mr. Roberts calm down.

BRAINSTORM

In the event that the customer has no basis for a complaint, you and your manager will need to decide whether to appease him or her. Pacifying customers who do not have valid complaints can become costly. Only your manager and the company's owner know what price the company can afford to pay to retain a customer.

Each case will be different; you will need to decide which customers are worth the effort. What are some situations that may arise in your business where a customer has no basis for his or her complaint? Think about the following questions and come up with some guidelines for handling these particular scenarios:

- Is this a one-time complaint, or is the customer a chronic complainer?

- What is your previous relationship with this customer?

- Does the customer do enough business with your company to make the aggravation worthwhile?

- Is this person a new customer you want to keep?

On occasion, you will need to make the tough decision that it is not cost effective to keep doing business with a high-maintenance customer. In these cases, your manager should make the final decision and handle the termination of the business relationship.

STEP 3
WHAT CAN I DO: RECTIFY THE SITUATION

You have investigated the situation and determined the cause of the problem. Now it is time to offer a solution. If you can rectify the problem to the customer's satisfaction, you get off easy: "Mr. Roberts, we have a service person who just called in. We're dispatching her to your home, and she'll be there within fifteen minutes."

More than likely, that is not going to be the case, and you are going to offer a solution your customer does not want to hear. What you say and how you say it will make a big difference in the customer's response.

Tell the Customer What You Are
Going to Do to Solve the Problem

Speak clearly and explain specifically what you will be able to do to rectify the problem. If you are handling a customer who is extremely upset or difficult, take a deep breath to calm your nerves, and think about what you will say before proceeding.

Focus on What You Can Do

Always focus on the positive and state what you are able to do rather than what you cannot do. In the case of Mr. Roberts, all the service people were already dispatched for the day, so sending someone out in the afternoon was not an option. What could Mike do for him? Before offering the solution, perhaps Mike could check with his dispatcher to see if he could schedule a service call for the first appointment the next morning. While this was not the solution that Mr. Roberts expected, it would narrow his wait time and give him preferential treatment that would make him feel better.

Offer Your Best Solution

This is not the time to offer something mediocre and begin a bartering session for a better solution. By offering the best you can do, you will sound more confident when presenting your solution. Putting yourself in the customer's shoes will help you understand how your solution may be received.

Never Assign Blame

When you offer your solution, do not fault the customer. How would you feel hearing, "If you had scheduled your appointment the first time you called, we would have come out." Statements like this will only make the customer defensive. When you are trying to help a difficult customer, blaming is never a wise approach. Similarly, never shirk responsibility by blaming another employee or department. Saying, "The first employee you spoke with messed up and should have scheduled your appointment," may relieve you from responsibility, but it does nothing to make the customer feel better. Always remember that to the customer, you are the company. Use "I" or "we" when referring to your company to show you are accountable.

Show Compassion

If the customer expresses dissatisfaction, let him or her know that you understand. Compassion and understanding can help mend a damaged relationship. You may not be able to fix the problem in the precise manner in which the customer would like, but at least you can show that you care.

Offer an Alternative Solution

If your best solution is not suitable to the customer, try to find something that will work. In the case of Mr. Roberts, if he cannot be home tomorrow morning, then offer a different time frame. If you do not know how to resolve a problem, ask for the customer's input as to what will work. Then, work together to come up with a realistic solution that is mutually acceptable.

PICTURE THIS...
THE RIGHT WAY TO RECTIFY THE SITUATION

"All our service people have already been dispatched for today but here's what I can do for you. I checked with our dispatch department to get you the earliest possible appointment. We can schedule you for the first appointment tomorrow. Someone will be out before nine."

"I want someone out today."

"I understand how you feel. If I waited all morning, I'd be upset too. I wish I could change what happened on your first phone call. I told my dispatcher what happened and asked if there was any way we could free someone up today. Unfortunately, we're completely booked and he said there is no chance we can do that. The best I can do is the first appointment tomorrow. I know this isn't what you were hoping for, but I tried my best for you."

"You say the person will be here before nine?"

"Yes, we already have you set up. I get in at eight tomorrow, and I'll personally follow up on this to make sure nothing goes wrong again."

"Well, Mike, I do appreciate your help. I guess tomorrow first thing is the best you can do."

"Yes, sir, it is."

How Did the Customer Feel?

Mr. Roberts appreciated Mike's honest and sincere answer. By speaking in a confident manner and focusing on what he could do, Mike made Mr. Roberts feel that he did his best. Mr. Roberts also appreciated Mike's understanding as to why he was upset.

TIP

Taking the time to adequately explain your solution will help you communicate more effectively. Tell the customer what you can do, and also explain why that is your best solution.

BRAINSTORM

What happens when a customer has a legitimate complaint that you cannot resolve to his or her satisfaction? What if Mr. Roberts still demanded an appointment today?

Discuss situations in which you were unable to find a satisfactory solution to a customer's problem, as well as how you should handle cases in which the customers' requests are impossible to satisfy. Talk about the following questions and come up with some "best solution" guidelines.

- What alternative solutions can you offer customers?

- What should you say to customers when you cannot find a satisfactory solution?

- At what point should you involve your manager (or owner)?

At times, no matter what you offer, your solution will not be acceptable. When this happens, make sure to say that you appreciate and understand the customer's point of view, that you did your best, and that you are sorry you were not able to work out a satisfactory solution.

STEP 4
WHAT CAN I SAY: RESTORE THE RELATIONSHIP

What you say next can go a long way in mending a broken relationship. When the bond in a personal relationship is damaged, you have to work hard to rebuild. The same goes for your business relationships.

Thank the Customer for Allowing You to Make Things Right

After you satisfactorily resolve a customer's problem, go one step further and thank them. You cannot take back what happened, but you can say something to let your customers know you value them as much as you value their business.

Tell What You Will Do to Avoid Future Problems

Now that you solved this customer's problem, what will keep it from happening again? Let your customer know that resolving this problem is important to your company. State what steps you will take to avoid future occurrences. Positively stating what you will do differently will give the customer renewed confidence in your company. When someone takes the time to acknowledge that there is a problem that can be fixed, it makes the customer feel valued. You send the message that your company truly does care about its customers. Plus, your customer will feel he is part of the solution.

Offer Some Sort of Compensation or Restitution

When your company is at fault and is the cause of the customer's problem, give the customer something more than is asked for, even if it is only a symbolic gesture. Doing this will not make the problem go away, but it will make the customer feel good about you and your company.

Make a Follow-Up Call or Visit

As a courtesy to your customer, follow up to make sure the solution was satisfactory. Think about this: Customers often take their business elsewhere without telling you they are dissatisfied. Every time this happens, you lose a valued customer. When customers take the time to tell you about a problem, they are giving you a valuable gift: the opportunity to improve.

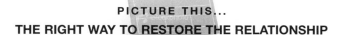

PICTURE THIS...
THE RIGHT WAY TO RESTORE THE RELATIONSHIP

"Mr. Roberts, thank you for giving us an opportunity to resolve your problem. I don't know what happened on your first phone call, but I am going to refer this to my manager so she can talk to everyone about it. That way, hopefully, we can avoid situations like this in the future."

The next afternoon Mike spoke with Mr. Roberts again:

"Mr. Roberts, this is Mike from ABC. I wanted to check back with you and make sure the service person was out this morning and fixed the problem."

"Yes, Mike, she was out first thing and everything is fine now. Thanks for calling me back."

How Did the Customer Feel?

Mr. Roberts felt valued when Mike thanked him for allowing him to fix the problem. By stating what he was going to do to avoid similar problems in the future, Mike conveyed the message that this company cares about satisfying its customers. Mr. Roberts was pleasantly surprised by the follow-up call, and his confidence in ABC was restored.

BRAINSTORM

Discuss appropriate forms of compensation or restitution to offer customers when your company caused a problem.

Think about your customers. What would be meaningful to them, and what is an appropriate form of compensation for your type of business to offer? Think, too, about which situations deserve an offer of compensation or restitution. Come up with different scenarios and how you can handle them. In addition, discuss who has the authority to approve compensation.

Some examples might be:

- Priority treatment for the next appointment.

- Credit toward the service charge or fees rendered.

- A gift certificate or discount toward a future purchase.

STEP 5
WHAT NEEDS TO BE DONE: FIX WHAT NEEDS TO BE FIXED

When you take care of a customer's problem to his or her satisfaction, you feel good, but unless you fix what went wrong, the same type of problem is likely to happen again. Repeatedly taking care of the same type of problems will only lead to frustration, both for you and your customers.

Analyze What Went Wrong

Sometimes this will not be easy. In Mike's case, for example, all he can determine is that a miscommunication occurred between Mr. Roberts and the previous employee. Further analysis will not provide a more specific understanding of this problem. Still, something can be done to avoid potential problems. Mike or his supervisor can address the issue in a meeting or by sending a memo to all employees. For example, the manager can ask employees to verify and clarify all appointments or recap the conversation before ending the contacts. If the first employee had said, "Mr. Roberts, I will make a note that you are going to call back to schedule your appointment," there might never have been a miscommunication in the first place.

Review Your Company's Policies and Procedures

If you have frequent customer complaints in one area, analyze your policies and procedures. Are there some aspects of your business operations that customers frequently complain about? Your primary goal should always be to make it easy for your customers to do business with your company. When it is easy for customers to do business with you, it is easier for you to satisfy them. As a customer service employee, you are in the position to know what makes things difficult for your customers.

Change to Make Things Better

When you are part of the solution, you will be more satisfied with the work you do. As the voice for your company and customers, you can make a difference.

BRAINSTORM

> If you cannot easily determine which areas make it difficult for your customers to do business with you, try this. Do a "walk through" of each step of a customer transaction. Look at your company from a customer's perspective. Discuss any areas that create difficulties for your customers. Try to devise ways to address those areas and rewrite your company's policies. Think about the following questions and come up with some guidelines:
>
> ■ How easy is it for customers to do business with you?
>
> ■ Which of your policies makes it difficult to satisfy your customers?
>
> ■ In what areas of your business do you get repeat complaints?

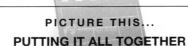

PICTURE THIS...
PUTTING IT ALL TOGETHER

"ABC Appliance Repair, this is Mike speaking."

"Mike, this is Mr. Roberts. My service contract number is ACH2234. I'm not very happy right now. I called early this morning, and you were supposed to send a service person before noon. Now it's twelve thirty and no one's showed."

"Mr. Roberts, I am so sorry that happened. I'll be happy to help you. You had a service appointment scheduled for this morning?"

"Yes, that's correct. I called first thing. The employee I spoke with told me she could send someone out this morning. I've been waiting all morning and no one came. I'm a busy person, and my time is valuable. I need someone out right away."

"I understand. I'll need to check our records to see what happened. Can you hold while I do that?"

"Yes, I'll hold."

"Mr. Roberts, thank you for holding. I checked our records, and again, I apologize that we weren't out this morning. When you spoke to the employee earlier, she was under the assumption that you needed to call back to schedule your appointment. We didn't hear back from you and therefore never scheduled the service call.

"All our service people have already been dispatched for today, but here's what I can do for you. I checked with our dispatch department to get you the earliest possible appointment. We can schedule you for the first appointment tomorrow. Someone will be out before nine."

"I want someone out today."

"I understand how you feel. If I waited all morning, I'd be upset too. I wish I could change what happened on your first phone call. I told my dispatcher what happened and asked if there was any way we could free someone up today. Unfortunately, we're completely booked and he said there is no chance we can do that. The best I can do is the first appointment tomorrow. I know this isn't what you were hoping for, but I tried my best for you."

"You say the person will be here before nine?"

"Yes, we already have you set up. I get in at eight tomorrow, and I'll personally follow up on this to make sure nothing goes wrong again."

"Well, Mike, I do appreciate your help. I guess tomorrow first thing is the best you can do."

"Yes, sir, it is. Thanks for being so understanding. I don't know what happened on your first phone call, but I am going to refer this to my manager so she can talk to everyone about it. That way, hopefully, we can avoid situations like this in the future."

Next afternoon:

"Mr. Roberts, this is Mike from ABC. I wanted to check back with you and make sure the service person was out this morning and fixed the problem."

"Yes, Mike, she was out first thing and everything is fine now. Thanks for calling me back."

All your difficult customers will not be as easy to satisfy as Mr. Roberts, but if you master the steps for handling difficult customers you will gain the confidence to positively handle any scenario. When you have confidence in your ability, it will be reflected in the way you deal with your customers. When you are confident in yourself, your customers will be confident in your ability to do your best for them.

The bottom line is that when you deal with customers, there are going to be problems. Whether the problem is caused by the customer or by the company, what is important in any contact with a difficult customer is what you do to resolve the problem and how valued you make the customer feel.

When a Customer Complains, Look at It as an Opportunity to Improve

Looking for opportunities to improve is always important; looking for opportunities to improve when business is down is not only important, it is vital. Think about this: If you don't satisfy your customers, they are going to find a business that does.

Do you know that the most common reason customers take their business elsewhere is mistreatment by frontline employees? And the sad news is that most of the time customers won't even complain. They just don't come back.

When customers take the time to complain, they are giving you a gift. They are giving you the chance to correct the situation. When you do so, you will not only save this customer, you also save others who would not take the time to tell you when something is wrong.

When you take the time to satisfy even the most difficult customers, you increase your chances of making it through difficult times.

- Make sure your attitude is never indifferent, but directed toward making a difference.

- Put yourself in your customers' shoes; try to see things from their perspective.

- Focus on the problem, not the person's attitude or behavior.

- Display empathy toward the customer's situation.

- Focus on what you can do.

K E Y   P O I N T S

Step 1: What Is Going On: Determine the Reason for the Problem

- Apologize.
- Assure the customer you are going to help.
- Restate the customer's opening statement.
- Listen carefully.
- Write down key details.
- Display empathy.
- Remain composed.

Step 2: What Caused the Problem: Identify the Root Cause

- Investigate the situation.
- Determine if the customer has a valid complaint.
- Apologize again if necessary.
- Explain what happened.

Step 3: What Can I Do: Rectify the Situation

- Tell the customer what you are going to do to solve the problem.
- Focus on what you can do.
- Offer your best solution.
- Never assign blame.
- Show compassion.
- Offer an alternative solution.

Step 4: What Can I Say: Restore the Relationship

- Thank the customer for allowing you to make things right.
- Tell the customer what you will do to avoid future problems.
- Offer some sort of compensation or restitution.
- Make a follow-up call or visit.

Step 5: What Needs to Be Done: Fix What Needs to Be Fixed

- Analyze what went wrong.
- Review company policies and procedures.
- Change to make things better.

PRACTICE LESSON

Refer to the customer contact example you wrote down at the beginning of the chapter.

Step 1: What is Going On: Determine the Reason for the Problem

Write down the customer's opening statement.

_____

_____

_____

Write a statement assuring this customer you are going to help. Restate the customer's opening statement to ensure your understanding

_____

_____

_____

How will you display empathy to let the customer know you understand?

_____

_____

_____

Step 2: What Caused the Problem: Identify the Root Cause

After investigating the situation, determine if the customer has a valid complaint. Need more time to investigate? If you need to call the customer back, explain how you will state the commitment.

_____

_____

_____

Write a statement explaining what happened.

_____

_____

_____

Step 3: What Can I Do: Rectify the Situation

Write a statement telling the customer what you can do to solve the problem.

_____

_____

_____

If the customer objects, write a statement offering empathy.

_____

_____

_____

Assume this customer is not satisfied with your resolution. Write an alternate solution you could offer.

_____

_____

_____

Step 4: What Can I Say: Restore the Relationship

Write a statement thanking the customer for allowing you to correct the problem.

_____

_____

_____

Tell the customer what you will do to avoid future problems.

_____

_____

_____

Was this problem caused by your company? Remember to leave your customer with a good impression of you and your business by offering some sort of compensation or restitution. What will you offer this customer?

_____

_____

_____

What will you say to the customer in your follow-up call?

_____

_____

_____

Step 5: What Needs to Be Done: Fix What Needs to Be Fixed

Think about this situation. Analyze what went wrong. What can you and your company do to avoid similar problems in the future? Write out what changes you will make.

_____

_____

_____

Remember, the important thing to keep in mind is to always strive to make it easy for your customers to do business with you.

D O I N G   I T   R I G H T !

My trips to a local Michael's Craft Store are usually to pick up specific items on my list. I know what I want and usually get in and out quickly. One visit, though, tested my patience and turned me into a difficult customer contact.

On that particular day, Michael's was offering a coupon special. If I spent a specific dollar amount, I would receive a discount on my total order. As I shopped, I added up the items I put in my cart to be sure I qualified for the discount. Samantha, the sales associate, rang up my order, but as soon as I swiped my credit card, I realized I had not received the discount.

When Samantha tried to credit me for the correct amount, her computer froze. She was unable to do anything. We couldn't move to another register because this one was already processing my credit card payment.

After a few minutes of pushing keys and waiting, Samantha called Will, the manager. When she told him what had happened, he immediately apologized (Samantha already had done so more than once). "No need to apologize," I countered, "it happens."

After he unsuccessfully tried unfreezing the computer, he looked at me resignedly and sighed. "We're going to have to call tech support. I am really sorry this happened, but since your credit card is processing we can't even ring you up on another register." Now, if you've ever had to call tech support, you know where this is headed.

First, let me explain that although I turned into a difficult customer contact, I did not become a difficult customer. I remained patient and respectful throughout the ordeal. I really felt sorry for Will and Samantha as she helplessly waited on hold and he nervously stood by. "Hey, it's OK." I sympathized. "Any time I have to call a tech support I know I'm going to be on the phone a while."

Finally, after about twenty minutes, the tech support person answered, rebooted her register, and she was able to complete my transaction. When she was doing that, Will excused himself and walked away, returning with a gift card for what happened. When I said he didn't need to do that, he commented, "It's the least I can do. This never should have happened and when it did it never should have taken this long to resolve."

In this situation, Samantha and Will did everything right. They both apologized immediately and the looks on their faces showed me they truly were sorry. They displayed empathy throughout for my having to wait so long. Most importantly, they restored my relationship by thanking me for being so understanding and by offering me the gift card for my trouble.

The outcome and moral of this story is simple. Because of the manner in which Samantha and Will handled my "difficult customer contact," I have become loyal, not only to Michael's Arts and Crafts, but to *my* Michael's. On a recent family visit out of state, I went into a local Michael's to pick up a product for my daughter. I saw something I was going to buy but didn't, telling myself that I'd get it at my Michael's when I got home. That is loyalty!

In business, problems are a fact of life. How you handle problems makes all the difference to your customers. Whether you are a small business or a large chain like Michael's, handling any situation to your customer's satisfaction and taking the extra step to restore the relationship will keep that relationship strong.

H O W   D O   I   M E A S U R E   U P ?

1. Do I apologize when a customer is upset or angry with my company? How well do I listen so that I can determine the reason for the problem?

   _____

   _____

2. After investigating the situation, do I apologize again if our company caused the problem and do I take the time to explain what happened?

   _____

   _____

3. When working to resolve the problem, how well do I focus on what I can do and always offer my best solution? If the customer is not satisfied with my recommendation, what do I do to find a workable solution?

   _____

   _____

4. Do I always remember to thank the customer for giving me the opportunity to make things right? What else do I do that sets me and my company apart and helps to restore our relationship?

    _____

    _____

5. Do I take the time to analyze what went wrong and follow up with my manager to make sure we change any areas that need improvement?

    _____

    _____

6. For any questions I answered no to, what can I do to improve how I handle difficult customer contacts?

    _____

    _____

PUTTING IT ALL TOGETHER

Hitting the Ground Running: Ready, Set, Go

**BEING GOOD AT WHAT YOU DO
MAKES DOING IT A PLEASURE**

You have covered a lot of ground in this book. Part I focused on putting your best face forward. You learned how to present yourself by using basic courtesies, communicating effectively, and building strong relationships. Part II focused on putting your customers first. You learned special skills to handle customers in person, on the telephone, through the Internet, and in self-service settings. You even learned how to handle difficult customers. Now, it is time to put it all together. You are on your way to giving great customer service. Where do you go from here?

CUSTOMER SERVICE IS BEING READY AND SET TO GO

Depending on your comfort level, you may either be ready to jump into the customer service fray with both feet, or you may only be ready to take your first steps. If you feel a little overwhelmed by all you have learned, you are not alone. Not everyone will be ready for that huge step. Do not feel embarrassed about first taking small steps. In fact, even if you feel confident that you are ready to apply everything you learned, it might be a good idea for you to focus on one area at a time so that you can turn each of these lessons into lifelong habits.

Review Your List of Learning Outcomes

If you feel unsure about any of the material, review the relevant chapters again. Go back over any sections of the training until you feel comfortable applying the material to your customer situations. If you still feel uncomfortable with any of the steps, discuss them with your manager. To get the most out of this training, it is important that you feel confident with the total package.

Start with the Basics

Focus on the way you present yourself when people are forming their first impressions. Get used to using courtesy words and phrases: please, thank you, excuse me, I'm sorry, yes, and so on. When you find yourself using these words without conscious effort, turn your attention to your attitude. Remember that your attitude includes how you talk to yourself, so always use positive words in your self-talk. Then, review the right way to handle ethical issues in Step 4 of Chapter 1 and form the habit of acting in an ethical manner in all situations.

When You Are Comfortable with the Basics, Focus on Communicating Effectively

Think before you speak, so you will say what you mean and mean what you say. Pay attention to the nonverbal messages you send by developing an awareness of your body language. Next, focus on your questioning skills. It may help to write down some sample open and closed questions that you will frequently use. Review them often so you will become comfortable using them. Remember that no matter what type of question a customer asks you, you should always try to give more than a one-word answer. Find ways to give your customers more than they ask for. When customers say no, find out the reason and offer the best solution based on each customer's needs. Finally, and most importantly, listen actively. As your company's communicator, listening is your most important skill to master. Unless you listen well, you are not going to know what is best for each customer.

Build Strong Relationships with Your Customers

Now that you have learned the nuts and bolts of communicating effectively, it is time to let your personality shine. Establish a rapport by being friendly and interested in your customers in order to find common ground. Once you establish a rapport, you will feel more comfortable interacting positively with your customers. Developing a comfort level will enable you to help each customer by identifying individual needs. When you do these things, you will make your customers feel valued. When customers feel valued, they are more likely to do repeat business with you and your company. The last thing you learned about relationships is that not all customers are the same. You learned how to deal with different personality types, people from different cultures, and people with disabilities. The most important thing to remember is to treat all your customers the way you like to be treated.

Practice Each of These Steps

Each step in the training is a building block you add to your customer service foundation. By the time you feel comfortable using all the principles learned in Part I, you have built a strong foundation. Practice using them not only at work, but also in your interactions with family and friends. Practice using them in situations in which you are the customer. Learning how to behave courteously and communicate well will help you build positive relationships in all areas of your life.

Put Your Customers First

Practicing the skills you learned in Part I will help you take a huge step in the right direction, whether you handle customers face-to-face, by telephone, in self-service settings, or through Web-based transactions. Forming a customer-first mindset is going to help you when you are confronted by a difficult customer. When you use courteous words, display appropriate behaviors, communicate effectively, and work to build strong relationships, you firmly cement your customer service skills so you can help any customer in any situation.

Warmly greeting customers helps them form a positive first impression, whether you are face to face with your customers or they are serving themselves. Conveying your willingness to help and maintaining a positive attitude helps you assist your customers whether you are e-mailing or speaking by phone. Finding the best solution for each customer and ensuring they are satisfied before ending your contacts will help you build solid relationships that result in loyal customers in every type of customer interaction.

Review These Steps Frequently

The more you use the principles you learned in Part I, the more comfortable and confident you will be when you apply them to the various types of customer contacts you learned in Part II. Reviewing the steps frequently helps you cement your foundation with a strong bond on which to build your customer service skills. If your foundation is built on anything but concrete principles, it can easily crumble at any time. You may fall into old habits. You may form poor habits. By reviewing each section of this training frequently, you guarantee you are maintaining a strong foundation of exceptional customer service habits.

YOUR CUSTOMER SERVICE TRAINING QUICK REFERENCE

Refer frequently to the quick reference list that follows to make sure you remember to follow all the lessons you learned.

The Basics

- First impressions matter.

- Courtesy counts.

- Attitude is everything.

- Do the right thing at all times.

Effective Communication

- Say what you mean and mean what you say.

- Pay attention to your body language.

- Use correct grammar.

- Ask the correct questions and answer the questions correctly.

- When the customer says no, find out why.

- Listen actively.

Relationship Building

■ Establish a rapport.

■ Interact positively with customers.

■ Identify customers' needs.

■ Make customers feel valued.

■ Maintain ongoing relationships.

■ Learn how to handle different types of customers.

Face-to-Face Contacts

■ Greet the customer.

■ Help the customer.

■ End the transaction by thanking the customer.

Telephone Contacts

■ Listen completely.

■ Greet the customer.

■ Help the customer.

■ End the call by thanking the customer.

E-Commerce Contacts

■ Learn what the e-customer is looking for: legitimacy, trust, and dependability.

■ Be accessible.

- Write carefully so that you write what you mean to write.

- When speaking with people in other countries, be mindful of cross-cultural etiquette.

Self-Service Contacts

- Greet the customer.

- Look for opportunities to help.

- End the transaction by thanking the customer.

Difficult Customer Contacts

- Determine the reason for the customer's problem.

- Identify the root cause.

- Rectify the situation.

- Restore the relationship.

- Fix what needs to be fixed.

10

Being the Best You Can Be: The Total Package

**ALWAYS LOOK FOR WAYS TO
MAKE YOURSELF BETTER**

Ready, set? Before you go, you need to take just one more step. You read an entire book devoted to helping you give exceptional customer service. This last chapter is devoted to you, to help you be the best you can be in everything you do.

CUSTOMER SERVICE IS
BEING THE BEST YOU CAN BE EVERY DAY

When you focus on being your best every day, good things happen. People will notice, respect you, and respond more positively. In turn, you will perform better at work, will seek out ways to give more of yourself to others, and find happiness and satisfaction in all you do.

Take Responsibility for Your Actions

You are the one person in charge of you. You control your actions, your performance at work, and your behavior. You make the decisions for and about yourself. When you make the decision to be your best at all times, you will strive to achieve your best, feel good about the choices you make, and feel good about yourself. When you feel good about yourself, you will reflect those feelings outward.

Become the Person You Want to Be

Create in your mind a positive vision of the person you want to become. If you have trouble seeing clearly, take time to focus on the qualities you want to personify. Envision the "you" you want to be. Picture yourself behaving this way, and keep this vision in your consciousness. Change your self-talk to reflect the new you. If your vision is to be more confident and self-assured, tell yourself that you are confident and self-assured, and then act this way. Initially it will be difficult and awkward, but the more you practice the easier it will become. Finally, these behaviors will be second nature and you will no longer need to act the part.

Set Goals for Yourself

What will it take for you to become the person you envision yourself being? Do you need to go back to school? Do you need to join an organization that fosters the qualities you wish to exemplify? Write down specific goals. There is something magical about writing your goals on paper. Once they are written, you will be more focused on finding ways to achieve them. If some of your goals are too big or long range, break them down into smaller, more manageable goals.

Keep Looking Forward

It is easy to get mired in the day-to-day grind. It is also easy to dwell on the past. When you look forward, it is easier to focus on your goals. Self-talk is important. You cannot change what happened, but next time you can do things differently. Change your self-talk to words that will help you view yourself more positively. Respect yourself by being respectful of the way you talk to yourself.

Measure Your Own Level of Performance

Periodically, answer the following questions. Do I feel good, both physically and mentally? Am I happy, both in my job and in my life? Do I look forward to each day, going to work and doing other activities? Am I proud of my efforts? If most of your answers were "yes," you are likely to perform well at work and are working toward achieving your goals. If most of your answers were "no," it is time for self-reflection. Look inward to figure out the cause and determine what you can do to improve yourself and your situation. This might mean rethinking your goals. It may be time to create a more realistic vision of your future so you can set goals that are attainable.

Keep Striving

To be your best means to keep striving to be even better. Improve your job skills. Ask questions to learn more. Try to learn something new every-day. Learn from every experience. When something bad happens, analyze why it happened to learn how to keep it from happening again. Do not repeat the same mistake twice. Ask for advice when you need help. Try to anticipate problems before they get out of hand. Be part of the solu-tion, rather than part of the problem. Give your all in everything you do and take the extra step for your customers, your family, and your friends.

Be a Good Listener

This theme has been stressed throughout the book because it is the most important quality you can develop. Listening completely is important, not only in work situations, but in everyday life situations. Being a good listener helps make you a good communicator. When you listen well, you become well informed. You learn more. You tune in to others. You know how to respond.

Enjoy Each Day

Have fun every day. Being the best you can be has a positive reward. You begin enjoying everything you do. Be positive. Find the good in others. When you encounter someone who is difficult to deal with, whether it is a customer, friend, or significant other, do whatever you can to make that person's day better. When you encounter a stranger, smile. Be grateful that you have this day. Be appreciative of those around you. Laugh often. Stay positive. Enjoy today.

ALWAYS BE YOUR BEST!

The Essence of Customer Service Is Having HEART

The character of a person is found deep in the heart.

- **Honesty:** Tell the truth. Do the right thing. Be trustworthy.

- **Empathy:** Put yourself in the other person's shoes. Listen. Care.

- **Appreciation:** Look for the good in people. Express gratitude.

- **Respect:** Show care, concern, and consideration.

- **Tolerance:** Rather than judging others, accept their differences.

INDEX